Essential First Steps for Parents of Children with Autism

TOPICS IN AUTISM

Essential First Steps for Parents of Children with Autism

HELPING THE LITTLEST LEARNERS

Lara Delmolino, Ph.D., BCBA-D & Sandra L. Harris, Ph.D.

Sandra L. Harris, Ph.D., series editor

Woodbine House ◆ 2013

All rights reserved. Published in the United States of America by Woodbine House, Inc., 6510 Bells Mill Road, Bethesda, MD 20817. 800-843-7323. www.woodbinehouse.com

Library of Congress Cataloging-in-Publication Data

Delmolino, Lara, author.
  Essential first steps for parents of children with autism : helping the littlest learners / by Lara Delmolino & Sandra L. Harris. -- First edition.
      pages cm. -- (Topics in autism)
  Includes bibliographical references and index.
  ISBN 978-1-60613-189-3 (alk. paper)
  1. Autistic children. 2. Autistic children--Education. 3. Parents of autistic children. I. Harris, Sandra L., author. II. Title.
  RJ506.A9D448 2014
  618.92'85882--dc23
                                                              2013038047

ISBN for print edition: 978-1-60613-189-3
ISBN for e-book edition: 978-1-60613-191-6
ISBN for PDF edition: 978-1-60613-190-9

Manufactured in the United States of America

10   9   8   7   6   5   4   3   2

For all of the families across more than four decades who have entrusted the faculty and staff of the DDDC with the welfare of their cherished child.

Table of Contents

Preface

We have written this book for the parents of toddlers, preschool-aged children, and youngsters through kindergarten age who have been diagnosed with autism spectrum disorder (ASD) or are considered at risk for a later diagnosis of that disorder. If you are a parent who is struggling to find information about how to help your child's development turn in a more typical direction, you will find answers to many of your questions.

We discuss a broad array of common parental concerns, including how to identify the early indicators that an infant or toddler may be on a trajectory that could lead to a diagnosis of ASD by the age of three. We also look at the specific behaviors of three- to five-year-olds who have been given a firm diagnosis of that condition. These so-called diagnostic features have been documented through research. They may well be the basis on which an expert or a team of experts in the field of ASD concluded that your child is at risk for an ASD diagnosis or clearly has the diagnosis.

Although our ability to make predictions for children younger than three years is not perfect, we have made a great deal of progress in developing diagnostic information within the last decade. This has markedly enhanced our ability to judge the likelihood that a child will ultimately be diagnosed with ASD. For children aged three and older, the decision is usually reliable when it is based on some of the most effective diagnostic methods currently available. We discuss diagnostic features for ASD, including an overview of the American Psychiatric Association's (2013) latest diagnostic system, in Chapter 1.

In Chapter 2, we review the research about treatments that are most helpful for children younger than six years of age. For children aged three to six, the research is much more extensive and rigorous than it is for children who are younger than three years. It is helpful for parents to be aware of what research tells us about effective interventions and also to understand the limits of current research. Where research on treatment is scant, as it still is for infants and toddlers, we describe how you can assess the impact of teaching methods on your own child and decide what appears to be helpful and what does not.

Chapter 3 addresses the important question of what you can do to help your child. For most parents, the most pressing concern is how they can make a difference in their child's development. Can you alter your child's developmental trajectory? We will focus on what you as a parent can do at home to support your child's development, as well as which professionals are likely to be of assistance to you and your child. It is also very important to know which treatments have not been proven effective so you can avoid wasting time on approaches that don't work. There are some widely promoted methods that have little evidence of benefit, and a few methods that have the potential to be harmful. In addition, we describe some of the teaching methods that have been demonstrated to be helpful for young children and explain where to get some help in learning these methods.

We devote the next four chapters to the topics of social skills, communication skills, increasing play, and basic self-help skills. These are all areas in which children with ASD often need considerable help in mastering the essentials. Chapter 9 explores how to address behavior problems and sensory issues in young children with ASD.

The final chapter discusses where you can find resources and help for yourself, your partner, your child with ASD, and the other children in your family. For parents, that includes not only learning to cope with the emotional stress of understanding and addressing your child's needs, but also finding the time to meet the multiple demands of maintaining a healthy and happy family life. We also consider where to get medical and educational information, how to find qualified people to work with you and your child, and what you can do if you need an occasional break from parenting demands.

You will find the book is rich in examples from the lives of some of the families with whom we have worked over the years. To protect their privacy, we have altered identifying information, but we have kept the crucial details that enable you to see how other parents have managed the challenges of raising their young child with ASD. So as not to imply that all children with ASD are the same gender, we have alternated our use of the personal pronouns he and she by chapter.

The two of us who have written this book together share 65 years of experience serving people with ASD and their families. Most of those years were at the Douglass Developmental Disabilities Center, our on-campus program at Rutgers University for people of all ages who have an ASD diagnosis. Over those years, we have witnessed a great many changes. Among the most exciting changes have been those enabling us to serve very young children in ways that have had a major positive impact on many of them. We hope the information we share in this book will empower you and other family members to help your young child reach his or her full potential.

Acknowledgments

We are both grateful for the support of our colleagues at the Douglass Developmental Disabilities Center. That includes Maria Arnold, Marlene Brown, Kate Fiske-Massey, Cat Francis, Barbara Kristoff, Robert LaRue, Debra Paone, Donna Sloan, Kim Sloman, and Barbara Weissenburger. We have an enduring sense of gratitude to the parents of the past forty-plus years who have entrusted their children to us and the Center and to the dedicated staff members who do such important work every day. We very much appreciate the generosity of the families who so graciously allowed us to use photographs of their children in this book. Susan Stokes, our wonderful editor at Woodbine House, is careful to ensure our technical language is translated into parent-friendly writing that is accessible to parents when they need it most.

Lara thanks Sandra for her inspiration and ongoing support. Lara is grateful to Chris, Brooke, and Erin, for the love and joy they bring to her life.

Sandra thanks Professor Emeritus Joseph Masling for his mentoring during graduate school, and later for the friendship that he and his wife, Annette, offered her. She also thanks her brother Jay, whom she loves, and who writes very fine books himself, as well as his wife, Maxine, who has so deeply enriched his life. Many thanks to her very best friend, Rhona Leibel, a professor of philosophy, who, over more than 50 years of friendship, has taught her a great deal and continues to do so in frequent phone conversations between New Jersey and Minnesota.

We both thank Professor Emerita Jean L. Burton, without whom there would not have been a DDDC; the members of the New Jersey State Federation of Women's Clubs who raised the money to give us our first building; our now deceased colleague, Jan Handleman, who was an important partner for many years in the operation of the DDDC; and the hundreds of Rutgers University undergraduate and graduate students who have been part of the DDDC since its founding.

Rutgers, The State University of New Jersey
Summer 2013

1 | Understanding Your Child's Diagnosis

The Hershey Family

Ken and Addie Hershey's daughter, Kate, was diagnosed with autism spectrum disorder at 22 months. Kate was the Hersheys' first child, and for some months they had been making excuses for her behaviors. She was tired, they told themselves, or she was just an irritable child. Maybe she had a hearing problem.

Ken and Addie were both only children and lived in a rural area where there were not many other toddlers, so they didn't have a very good basis for comparing Kate to other children her age. Kate did use some words and liked to stack blocks one on top of the other. But when her block tower got too tall and fell over, she often went into a rage and kicked the blocks and her parents as well. It took her a long time to get over her intense tantrums. In addition, she often appeared to ignore her parents.

At Christmas time, the Hersheys flew to Baltimore to stay with Addie's family for the holidays. The flight was terrible, with Kate crying and screaming for much of the time and other passengers glaring at them for not knowing how to quiet their daughter. When they got to her parents' home, Addie tried to put Kate down for a nap, but again, she screamed for a long time. Finally, exhausted, Kate fell asleep for a short while. When she woke up, she was very upset and tearful again. None of her toys interested her; she pushed her parents away and hid behind the sofa when her grandparents reached out to her.

Addie's parents were dismayed to learn that Kate used her words very rarely and did not want to interact with anyone. She never even looked at her grandparents. Addie and Ken told them that Kate spent most of her time building block towers and crying when they fell over.

Addie's mother, Clara, was a special education teacher. She watched her granddaughter closely for a couple of days before she said anything to Ken and Addie. Then she told them she thought there was something seriously wrong with Kate; she recommended they get a good diagnosis of what was going on with their child and enroll her in an early intervention program. At first, Ken and Addie were annoyed that Clara was "meddling," but when they talked in private, they realized that Clara might be right.

When Ken and Addie returned to their farm after the trip to Baltimore, they went online and visited the website of a program for "problem toddlers" at the university hospital. The hospital was two hours away, but they knew they had to get an expert opinion about Kate and that the university would probably have very knowledgeable staff members. They made an appointment, filled out the forms they were sent, and arrived at the hospital on the scheduled day. As they watched the developmental experts evaluate their daughter, they recognized that Kate did some things fairly well, but she rarely used any of her words and never looked at any of the people in the room. When the speech and language pathologist called Kate's name from behind her, Kate ignored her. When Addie did the same, she appeared to ignore her mother as well.

At the end of the evaluation, the team met with Ken and Addie while one of the volunteers looked after Kate. Although Ken and Addie had both heard of autism, neither one of them knew the terms the pediatric neurologist used. He said that Kate appeared to be on a developmental path that would eventually lead to her being diagnosed as a relatively high functioning girl with autism spectrum disorder. She had some language and had excelled at a few things on the intelligence testing, such as assembling puzzles and making a block train. On the other hand, she avoided interactions with other people as much as she could and got upset when she had to change rooms or move on to new tasks. She appeared to have good intellectual potential, but would need a lot of help in developing social skills and learning to cope with the anxiety that seemed to overwhelm her when unpredictable things happened.

Introduction

If you are reading this book, you probably have been told or suspect that your child has autism spectrum disorder (ASD). But you may still have many questions about how professionals can recognize these problems in very young children and what can be done to help your child grow toward a more typical developmental path.

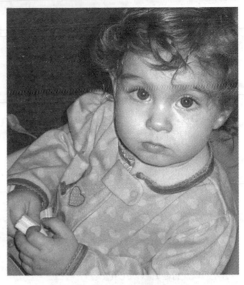

Twenty or thirty years ago, it is unlikely that anyone would have considered making a diagnosis of ASD until your child was at least three years old, and often not until the age of five or six. In the case of the Hershey family, Ken and Addie were fortunate to have Kate's diagnosis shortly after her second birthday. Years ago, even after parents got the diagnosis, there was little they could do to help their young child. Fortunately, increasing numbers of children are getting a diagnosis by 12 to 18 months (and sometimes even earlier). In addition, we now have some highly effective treatment methods that have benefitted many young children. We will discuss those later in this book.

Terminology

You may have heard a number of terms used to describe your child. People may have told you that he has autism, autistic disorder, autism spectrum disorder (ASD), or pervasive developmental disorder. People may also have considered whether the correct diagnosis was Asperger's disorder (or syndrome) or pervasive developmental disorder-not otherwise specified (PDD-NOS) rather than autistic disorder. Any child who has previously been given a diagnosis of one of these categories is now considered to have autism spectrum disorder, and you will probably hear professionals use that term more often in the next few years (American Psychiatric Association, 2013).

All of the older professional diagnostic terms overlap. That is, they involve some of the same behaviors, but they do not all mean the same thing. Our goal in this first chapter is to help you understand why your child has been given a diagnosis of autism spectrum disorder. To do that, we will share information with you about the early behaviors that may signify a child has ASD and how the development of children with ASD differs from that of typically developing children.

Our first objective is to give you some information about the book that is widely used in the United States to help mental health professionals diagnose autism spectrum disorders—the DSM-5. The information in this book is coordinated with the World Health Organization's publication, the *International Classification of Disease* (ICD). This allows the diagnostic codes that are used in professional reports and for health insurance purposes to be consistent between the two codes.

Autism as a "Spectrum" Disorder

The term *autism spectrum disorder* became an official diagnosis in the spring of 2013 when the American Psychiatric Association published the new edition of the *Diagnostic and Statistical Manual of Mental Disorders*, the DSM-5. The American Psychiatric Association published the first diagnostic manual in 1952, and each successive edition has grown in scope and complexity. The DSM-5 does not just include information about ASD, but about a wide variety of other mental health categories.

Although many experts in the field have used the term "autism spectrum disorder" for some time, this did not become an official diagnosis until the publication of DSM-5 in 2013. This term has become popular in educational and other circles in the past decade or so.

The new edition of the DSM eliminated the different diagnostic terms that had been used for various manifestations of ASD-related conditions. These older terms included autistic disorder, Asperger's disorder, pervasive developmental disorder-not otherwise specified, and childhood disintegrative disorder. These terms were often used to indicate the relative severity of a child's diagnosis. For example, children with the mildest behaviors were often diagnosed with Asperger's disorder or PDD-NOS. Those with the most significant disabilities were often diagnosed with autistic disorder, or if the onset of symptoms was later, childhood disintegrative disorder. These separate categories have been eliminated because many professionals now believe that autism encompasses a *spectrum* of behaviors and intellectual abilities. That is, the severity of any given behavior or characteristic of autism can be present in a mild to severe degree in any given individual.

Table 1-1	The DSM-5 Autism Spectrum (American Psychiatric Association, 2013)

1. Deficits in social communication & interaction
2. Restricted, repetitive behavior
3. Each rated on a 3-point continuum from "Requiring Very Substantial Support" to "Requiring Support"
4. Identify intellectual disability; language impairment; and medical or genetic features

In order to receive a diagnosis of autism spectrum disorder, a child must have behaviors that fall into two broad categories. These are:

1. **Deficits in Social Communication and Social Interaction.**
   This category refers to many challenges in social communication and interaction that are an integral part of having an ASD. You may have noticed that your child does not use gestures effectively, may not follow your gaze, and/ or may not engage in back-and-forth verbal or nonverbal interactions. For example, he may not participate in a game of "Pat-a-Cake."

2. **Restricted, Repetitive Patterns of Behavior and Interests.**
   This category encompasses some of the behaviors you may see in your own child and that you may consider "stubborn" or "unusual," such as eating only a few foods, getting upset if you don't follow his bedtime routine precisely, or lining up his toys in a very specific order.

In addition, the professional who makes the diagnosis must determine how severe these deficits or behaviors are in order to describe where the child falls on the diagnostic continuum. Each of these criteria is rated on a 3-point scale, with Level 3 being the most severe and Level 1 being the least severe.

To be diagnosed with an ASD, the child must meet both the criteria for #1 and #2. If he only meets the criteria for #1, he might have Social Communication Disorder, described in the box on page 13.

According to the DSM-5, the diagnosing professional also needs to specify whether the child has an intellectual disability and whether his social behavior is impaired relative to his intelligence. In addition, the diagnostician reports whether ASD is accompanied by a language

impairment. If a child's verbal ability is limited, but appropriate for his intellectual level, ASD might not be the appropriate diagnosis. Instead, the child may have a more global delay, such as occurs with a sole diagnosis of intellectual disability (formerly known as mental retardation). On the other hand, if language development has lagged behind intellectual ability, ASD should be considered. The DSM-5 also calls for identifying whether ASD is linked to a known medical or genetic condition such as a seizure disorder (medical) or fragile X syndrome (genetic disorder).

What Are the Earliest Indicators of Autism Spectrum Disorders?

Some very good research in recent years has enabled us to recognize the early signs of autism spectrum disorder in infants and toddlers. Professionals use the term *early phenotype* to refer to the behaviors of young children that indicate they ultimately will be diagnosed with ASD. (The term "phenotype" is a technical word that refers to the observable features of a condition.) For example, if a child resists changes in the environment from an early age, it suggests he is at risk for ASD. Likewise, if the child is not interested in looking at his parent as part of communication, that is also suggestive of that risk. There are two types of research that can identify these early behaviors—the prospective and retrospective approaches.

In the *prospective* (looking forward) approach, a large group of infants and toddlers who have not been diagnosed with ASD are studied. During the study, the children are repeatedly assessed for many different signs that could potentially predict ASD. Then, between 24 and 36 months of age, they are evaluated to determine whether they have ASD.

The advantage to using a prospective research design is that scientists can collect videotapes and other assessment data well before a child begins to exhibit the later, more widely recognized symptoms of ASD.

Prospective research is often done with the baby siblings of children who are already known to have ASD. That's because these babies are more likely to have ASD themselves than are babies in a random sample. The Centers for Disease Control and Prevention, which monitors the frequency with which ASD occurs in the United States, has found that the probability of any given family having a child with ASD is about 1 percent. In contrast, if parents have one child with ASD, there is a 2 to 18 percent chance that their next child will also have ASD. This increased frequency of ASD in families is the basis for studying the baby siblings of children who have been identified as having ASD (Ozonoff et al., 2011).

An alternative to the prospective study is for scientists to gather information from parents whose children were diagnosed with ASD at age 3 years or older. Researchers ask parents to reflect back on their child's earlier development and describe specific aspects of his behavior such as speech, social behavior, and repetitive behaviors. This research design is called a *retrospective* (looking back) approach. Although it is useful, it is vulnerable to all of the forgetting and other memory challenges we face in looking back at our lives. Fortunately, prospective and retrospective research studies often converge in their findings, which gives us considerable confidence in the results of these studies.

Table 1-2 | Different Approaches to Studying ASD

Retrospective: Asks parents to recall facts about their child's early behavior after the child has been diagnosed with ASD. Can also include reviewing early videos of the child.

Prospective: Follows the baby from shortly after birth. Ongoing videos of activities and assessments are made. Often involves study of the baby siblings of children already diagnosed with ASD.

Typical Child Development

It is difficult to understand what makes development unusual in children with ASD without knowing how development unfolds in typical youngsters. We will therefore discuss how children typically develop in the first few years of life before describing in detail in how children with autism spectrum disorder develop. In particular, how do social and communication skills progress in typically developing children and how is this different than in children with ASD? As you read about typical child development, remember that there is considerable variability in the rate at which typical children develop. While there is an age at which most children have acquired a given developmental skill, some children learn the skill earlier and some later than the average age (Bishop et al., 2008).

One of the fascinating aspects of typical child development is that babies arrive in the world already "programmed" to respond to social stimulation. For example, newborn babies like to look at pictures of faces more than at non-face patterns, and they pay more attention to speech than non-speech sounds, according to a summary of research on social development in young children (Bishop, Luyster, Richler, & Lord, 2008). In fact, even before birth, infants-to-be begin to learn their native language as they hear their mothers' vowel sounds (Moon et al., 2012).

Throughout the first year of life, a baby's vocalizations become increasingly refined and more "speech-like." Many children can say a few words by their first birthday. The cooing, babbling, grunting, and first words of infancy become the basis for pleasurable interchanges with caretakers. From very early in their child's life, parents are often richly rewarded for talking to their child. At first, they are rewarded by their child gazing at their face and eyes. A little later they are rewarded by his smiles and laughter, and then by vocal interchanges. The reciprocity of these interchanges not only creates the pattern for turn taking in conversation, but also builds a matrix for an array of interpersonal exchanges such as peek-a-boo and pat-a-cake in which parent and child have reciprocal roles. Language and social behavior continue to support one another across the course of child development.

Partway through the first year of life, a typical baby begins to recognize a few words, including his name, the names of familiar games such as pat-a-cake, and the word "no," although setting and tone of voice also help with this recognition. By his first birthday, a baby can point to some body parts and respond to spoken invitations to play familiar games with much less contextual support than needed earlier. By his second birthday, the baby can understand many words outside of the immediate context. At around one year of age, children can speak a few words, and by 18 months, most of them are making impressive gains in the use of speech. Between 18 and 24 months, the typically developing child begins to combine words into two- or three-word phrases.

Table 1-3	Language Development in the Early Years
Prenatal	Recognize maternal vowel sounds
Newborn	Attend more to speech than non-speech sounds
12 months	May say a few words
18 months	Make rapid gains in using single words
24 months	Combine words into short phrases

One very important social skill that supports the development of language in very young children is *joint attention.* In its most obvious form, joint attention is the "Wow, look at that sunset" phenomenon in which I look at the sunset, point at it, and turn toward you to make sure you are following my gesture and looking at the sunset also.

There are two aspects of joint attention: 1) responding to another person's initiation and 2) making initiations to others. To respond to joint attention, we have to be able to track the other person's gaze or gesture. When we initiate joint attention by words or gesture, we are deliberately communicating to another person our wish for him to share our visual experience. Both response and initiation of joint attention emerge during the first year of life. By shortly after their first birthdays, many typically developing children are fairly skillful at following an adult's gaze or gesture, and by 18 months, they can track the target of a parent's gaze even if it is behind them.

What Is Different about Children with Autism Spectrum Disorder?

Deficits in Social Communication & Interaction

Autism spectrum experts Fred Volkmar, Katarzyna Chawarska, and Ami Klin (2008) have found that the *earliest parental concerns* about their toddler's development include:

- delays in speech and language,
- problems with social responsiveness,
- medical problems, and
- what they call "nonspecific" difficulties with the child's sleeping, eating, and appropriate attending.

These difficulties are nonspecific in that they are not unique to autism spectrum disorders. They are found in typically developing children as well as in those with other developmental challenges. Another early concern for some parents is that their child no longer seems to be making developmental progress or has lost some skills he had previously learned. For example, a child who had started to use some single words may stop learning new words and may stop using some of the words that were already in his repertoire.

In their summary of the research, Volkmar and his colleagues (2008) noted that by their first birthday, children who will later be diagnosed as having autism spectrum disorder (ASD) have a number of *delays in social skills*. These may include:

- poor eye contact,
- limited interest in social interaction and other people's smiles,
- fewer gestures,
- failure to respond to their name,
- difficulties with imitation, and
- speech and language delays.

Other researchers have found that children at risk for a later diagnosis of ASD become more difficult to engage socially between 6 and 12 months of age. They also become more irritable and less accepting of intrusions by others, exhibit more negative emotions (by having tantrums or crying), and do not have effective self-soothing (self-comforting) skills (Bryson et al., 2007). In other words, at some point after 6 months of age, many children who will later be diagnosed with ASD become increasingly less accessible to the input of others.

Why does it matter how open a child is to others' input? One important reason is that a baby's *temperament* has been shown to be related to early language development. One group of researchers (Bishop et al., 2008) described several studies focusing on children's temperament and language skills. These studies showed that children who were more adaptable and persistent and had a more positive mood when they were 13 months old had more useful words when they were 20 months old, compared to children who were less adaptable and good humored. Research suggests that this is because parents are likely to interact more with cheerful, happy children than with crankier children. This higher level of engagement may increase a child's language learning opportunities (Bishop et al., 2008).

The difficulties very young children with ASD experience with social and language skills continue and may intensify as they grow older. According to Dr. Volkmar and his colleagues (2008), research has shown that *predictors of an ASD diagnosis for children between 24 and 36 months* include:

- continued difficulties with eye contact,
- little interest in simple turn-taking games,
- a preference for solitude, and
- an indifference to their parents' reactions to their activities.

Another common sign of ASD is a *delay in speech and motor imitation.* For example, typically developing children watch what their parents do and then try to do it themselves. A parent might roll a toy car and say "Zoom, Zoom," and the typically developing child will take another car and do the same without any prompting. The failure to watch what their parents or other children are doing and then imitate that action cuts children with ASD off from a valuable way of acquiring new skills. Most children with ASD have to be taught how to imitate. They don't simply imitate others because they find it interesting to do so.

In addition, young children with ASD often do not show much interest or engagement in *symbolic play*. A typically developing child in this age range might pretend that a block is a car or a bowl is a hat. In contrast, a child with ASD usually plays in very concrete ways, such as by stacking blocks or lining up cars, rather than using items in a symbolic way.

Problems with *using gestures* to communicate become increasingly obvious as children with ASD get older. We learn most of our gestures by watching what other people do and then doing the same—whether it be shrugging, pointing, or clapping our hands. Waving "bye-bye" is a good example of a simple gesture that typically developing children learn quickly, but may take some time for children with ASD to master.

It is also hard to overlook the difficulties that children with ASD have in responding to their own names. Many parents wonder if their child is deaf when he repeatedly fails to response to his name. However, most children with ASD do respond to other sounds that are linked to items that interest them, such as a wind-up toy that makes music or the rustling of a bag of potato chips.

The failure to develop age appropriate *joint attention* is also quite apparent by this age. Unlike typically developing children, who will track the direction of a parent's eye gaze or look at an object when a parent points it out, children with ASD are slow to respond to others' joint attention gestures or to try to point out items of interest to their parents. They are also less likely to bring items to their parents simply to show them and share their interest. But they may bring objects to others as a means of requesting that they be fixed or opened.

Restricted, Repetitive Behavior

As discussed above, restricted and repetitive behaviors are integral to the diagnosis of ASD. There is some debate, however, about when these behaviors cease to be "normal" and take on diagnostic significance. After all, typical young children have many repetitive (or *stereotypic*) behaviors (Bishop et al., 2008). For example, babies commonly kick their feet, wave their arms, bounce, and rock their bodies. Likewise, toddlers and preschoolers often enjoy lining up their toys, following routines at bedtime, and having the same book read to them countless times. What makes the repetitive behaviors of children with ASD different?

One important factor may be the ages when these behaviors occur (Bishop et al.). Over time, most babies do less and less of the stereotyped motor behaviors that are so common between 6 months and 9 months of age. Similarly, the compulsive rituals of toddlers and preschool-age children peak between 2 and 3 years of age and then decline to very low levels between 4 and 6 years of age. In contrast, the *ritualized and compulsive behaviors* of children with ASD usually increase with age. For example, they may insist on following specific routines such as always drinking juice from a blue cup, or turning left out of the driveway to go to Grandma's house, or wearing the same yellow dress every day.

It is also important to look at the variety and frequency of *ritualized behaviors*. Most typically developing young children have only a couple of these behaviors and will gladly include others in their routines. For example, a child who likes to line up all his toy cars will be happy to have his brother help line them up and then will play with the cars with his brother. In contrast, children at risk for ASD have many more ritualized behaviors and often resist other people's attempts to intrude on their rituals.

Restricted behaviors often involve a focus on a specific object. For example, one preschooler was fascinated by sewer drains and would stop to look at every one when his parents took him on a walk. Another child was preoccupied with air conditioners and would run

Can a Child Have ASD without Repetitive or Restricted Behaviors?

What if your child has many of the difficulties with social and communication skills described above but does not have repetitive or restrictive behaviors? Is he likely to be diagnosed with ASD?

According to the DSM-5, no. Instead, he might have something called **Social (Pragmatic) Communication Disorder**. Children who have problems using and understanding social and gestural communication, but do not demonstrate behavioral rigidity or resistance to change, may be eligible for this new diagnosis rather than autism spectrum disorder.

Youngsters with this diagnosis have problems using language appropriate to the context in which they are trying to communicate. They don't engage in the usual give and take of communication, nor can they always rephrase something to help a listener understand what they are saying. They also have problems in figuring out when a speaker is being funny or is using an idiom to communicate.

DSM-5 indicates that until a child is 4 to 5 years of age and would usually be able to communicate effectively, it is difficult to diagnose Social Communication Disorder. That is older than the age at which ASD can now be diagnosed.

away from his parents to inspect air conditioners in the windows of strangers' houses. We knew another boy who would stare at the leaves on a shrub with a sober expression that led his parents to wonder if he had the potential to be a botanist. Yet another youngster took one of us by the hand with what appeared to be impressive social skills until it turned out that he had an interest in digital watches, not in social interaction. Older or more verbal children with ASD may demonstrate their restricted interests by talking incessantly about their topic of interest.

Formal Assessment of Autism Spectrum Disorder

If you are concerned that your child may have autism spectrum disorder, or if he has been diagnosed with ASD, but you question whether this is the right diagnosis, what can you do? It makes good sense to have your child evaluated by experts who have a lot of experience making this diagnosis. If you have lingering doubts after one

person or team has given you the diagnosis, it is also reasonable to seek a second opinion so that you can satisfy yourself that the initial diagnosis was accurate.

If you share your concerns with your child's pediatrician, he or she should be able to refer you to specialists or programs that can assess your child. If you like, you can have the assessment done free of charge through your local early intervention program, as explained in Chapter 4. Or you can contact professionals directly and pay for an assessment yourself or through your health insurance if you have a policy that includes services for ASD.

The diagnosis of ASD in a very young child may be made by a child psychiatrist, a pediatric neurologist, a developmental pediatrician, or a clinical psychologist. Frequently, these professionals work in a team with a social worker, speech and language pathologist, and learning disabilities specialist. For example, at our Center we have psychologists, speech and language specialists, and learning consultants who can be called upon to provide a diagnosis and in-depth assessment of the child's abilities and challenges. The team members all contribute to a report that has sections summarizing the observations of each professional and a set of recommendations for intervention.

What Happens in an Assessment?

In determining whether your child has, or is at risk for, autism spectrum disorder, the professional or team of professionals will ask you many questions, observe your child, and administer a number of assessment tools. They will compare your child's behaviors and abilities with norms for typically developing children, check to see how many of the known signs of ASD he has, and consider other reasons for differences and delays in his development.

Depending on his age and abilities, this process may take several hours and be spread across several days, or it may take only part of one day. Especially with very young children, it is important that they not become so tired that it affects their ability to respond. Professionals who are experienced with young children will often stop a testing session if it appears that your child needs to take a break, or suggest that you come back another day to finish the evaluation.

Assessment Tools Specific to ASD

One major contribution to our ability to diagnose young children early and accurately was the development of two assessment tools that are the "Gold Standard" of ASD diagnosis—the *Autism Diagnostic Interview Revised* (ADI-R) and the *Autism Diagnostic Observation Schedule*.

ADI-R: The *Autism Diagnostic Interview Revised* (ADI-R; Lord, Rutter, & LeCouteur, 1994) is an intensive and extensive parent interview. The questions focus on a number of areas related to the symptoms of ASD. For example, there are questions about your child's interest in you, his behavioral flexibility, and how he communicates. In the hands of a well-trained professional and with the cooperation of parents, this is a valuable interview for determining whether a child has ASD. The ADI-R is useful for children with a mental age of 2 years or higher.

Autism Diagnostic Observation Schedule: This diagnostic instrument from Western Psychological Services (Lord, Rutter, DiLavore, & Risi, 1999) has modules for people of varying ages and ability levels. It creates a series of interactions between the professional and the child to explore specific behaviors that are found in ASD. These domains include speech and language, social interaction, play behavior, and stereotypic or repetitive actions. For example, the examiner might give your child a snack in a sealed box that requires adult help to open, and wait to see if your child makes any gesture or sound to ask for help and whether he uses eye contact along with his request.

As we noted at the beginning of this chapter, parents are usually present during the evaluation of a young child. These assessments are useful for toddlers and older children as well. There are even modules for adolescents and adults.

Both the ADOS and the ADI-R can be used in a consistent and reliable way by people who have been trained to administer and score them (Delmolino, LaRue, Fiske, Martins, & Harris, 2007). When used together, they are a highly effective way to identify children with ASD. If you have been told that your child has ASD and no one has administered one or both of these assessments, you may want to seek out a professional who is trained in their use and can provide that service. Usually the ADOS and the ADI are administered by clinical psychologists, but some physicians, including developmental pediatricians, have been trained in their use as well.

IQ Tests

The cognitive skills of typically developing children tend to remain relatively stable over time. That means children continue to acquire new knowledge and problem solving abilities at a consistent rate as they mature. For most children, tests that measure "IQ" (intelligence) show stability over time. That is, if a very young child's intelligence is measured in the average range or above average range, it will tend to remain within that range over his lifetime.

The same is not true for many children with ASD. Two researchers who have studied changes in cognitive functioning in young children found that rates of intellectual progress between years two and three are highly variable in children on the autism spectrum (Chawarska &

Bearss, 2008). In about half of children with ASD, intelligence test scores decrease over time or remain at a previously measured relatively low level of intelligence.

In a prospective (looking forward) study following baby siblings from 6 months to 24 months of age, another group of researchers (Bryson et al., 2007) found that IQ scores of one subgroup of children decreased from the average or near average range to a level of severe impairment, and one child went from being "impossible to test" at 12 months to severely cognitively impaired at 24 months. A smaller group of children, however, maintained roughly the same average or near average IQ over time.

Given the dramatic changes in cognitive functioning among a large number of toddlers at risk for ASD, many of whom were ultimately diagnosed with ASD, you will want a psychologist to administer an intelligence test such as the *Mullen Scales of Early Learning* (1997) to your child. These tests will help both you and your child's teachers identify areas of relative strength and weakness and come up with appropriate teaching objectives. It is a good idea to repeat that test several times in the early years. The *Mullen* can be used with children from 2 days of age to 69 months and has been standardized on typically developing children. This test can be used to assess a child's gross motor, visual reception, fine motor, expressive language, and receptive language abilities.

Alternatively, many psychologists use the *Bayley Scales of Infant and Toddler Development* (Bayley, 2005), which is useful for assessing the development of children from 1 to 42 months. Both the *Bayley* and the *Mullen* tests are widely used by researchers who are studying very young children suspected of ASD to track their progress over time. These assessments can help you and the professionals who are working with your child realistically evaluate your child's progress over time.

You and your child's teachers and therapists can then make adjustments to his teaching program to ensure he makes optimal progress with the help of intensive services. It is important to remember that regardless of tested intelligence, all children have strengths as well as weaknesses and are able to make progress with appropriate treatment.

Measures of Adaptive Functioning

Unlike typically developing age peers, children with ASD tend to have difficulty transferring their daily living skills (adaptive skills) such as dressing or using the toilet from one setting to another (Chawaraska & Bearss, 2008). For example, a child may urinate in the toilet at school, but not use that skill at home. Children with ASD also master these skills at a slower rate than other children their age, and even more slowly than their intelligence test scores suggest they could learn them.

You may want to systematically measure your child's adaptive skills as part of the periodic check on his developmental progress. One good way to do this is with the *Vineland Adaptive Behavior Scales II Caregiver Rating Form* (Sparrow, Cicchetti, & Balla, 2005). This scale consists of a series of questions for parents about their child's independence in activities of daily living including communication skills, self-help, socialization, and motor skills.

Both the *Mullen Scales of Early Learning* and the *Vineland II* are commonly used in research to measure changes in young children with ASD from pre- to post-treatment, and, like the ADOS and the ADI-R, are well validated.

Other Tests

If a diagnosis is ambiguous or if alternative explanations for your child's behaviors need to be explored, your child may be referred to other specialists for testing. For example, if there are legitimate concerns about his hearing, you may be referred to an audiologist who is expert in assessing children's hearing. If you have observed behaviors that suggest some seizure activity may be present, a pediatric neurologist might do an EEG to determine whether a specific kind of seizure is contributing to your child's behavior and is a more appropriate diagnosis than ASD.

Summary

The most recent guidelines for making a diagnosis of autism spectrum disorder were released by the American Psychiatric Association in 2013. The new criteria call for making the diagnosis of ASD if a child has specific difficulties in social behavior and restricted, repetitive behavior. The diagnosis is made on a continuum reflecting the severity of the child's symptoms.

Thanks to major advances in the study of very young children, we can now recognize some of the signs that a child may be at risk for a diagnosis of ASD by the time he reaches his third birthday. If you observe these signs in your child, the best way to help him develop new skills and more appropriate behaviors is to seek a diagnosis and get treatment recommendations from experts in the treatment of children with ASD. If the diagnosis turns out to be something other than ASD, these experts can help set you on the path to the treatment methods that are fitting for your child.

References

American Psychiatric Association. (2013). *Diagnostic and statistical manual of mental disorders* (5th ed.). Arlington, VA: APA.

Bayley, N. (2005). *Bayley scales of infant and toddler development* (3rd ed.). Livonia, MN: Pearson Assessments.

Bishop, S. L., Luyster, R., Richler, J., & Lord, C. (2008). Diagnostic assessment. In K. Chawarska, A. Klin, & F. R. Volkmar (Eds). *Autism spectrum disorders in infants and toddlers: Diagnosis, assessment, and treatment* (pp.23-49). New York, NY: Guilford Press.

Bryson, S. E., Zwaigenbaum, L., Brian, J., Roberts, W., Szatmari, P., Rombough, V., & McDermott, C. (2007). A prospective case series of high-risk infants who developed autism. *Journal of Autism and Developmental Disorders, 37*, 12-24.

Centers for Disease Control and Prevention. (2012). *Prevalence of autism spectrum disorders (ASDs) among multiple areas of the United States in 2008* (Community report from the Autism and Developmental Disabilities Monitoring Network). Retrieved from CDC website: http://www.cdc.gov/ncbddd/autism/documents/addm-2012-community-report.pdf

Chawarska, K., & Bearss, K. (2008). Assessment of cognitive and adaptive skills. In K. Chawarska, A. Klin, & F. R. Volkmar (Eds). *Autism spectrum disorders in infants and toddlers: Diagnosis, assessment, and treatment* (pp.50-75). New York, NY: Guilford Press.

Delmolino, L., LaRue, R., Fiske, K., Martins, M., & Harris, S. L. (2007). Pervasive developmental disorders. In M. Hersen & J. C. Thomas (Eds.). *Comprehensive handbook of interviewing* (pp.196-211). Thousand Oaks, CA: Sage.

Lord, C., Rutter, M., & LeCouteur, A. (1994). Autism diagnostic interview revised: A revised version of a diagnostic interview for caregivers of individuals with possible developmental disorders. *Journal of Autism and Developmental Disorders, 24,* 659-685.

Lord, C., Rutter, M., DiLavore, P. C., & Risi, S. (1999). *Autism diagnostic observation schedule — WPS edition (ADOS-WPS).* Los Angeles: Western Psychological Services.

Moon, C., Lagercrantz, H., & Kuhl, P. (2012). Language experienced in utero affects vowel perception after birth: A two-country study. *Acta Paediatrica.* doi: 10.1111/apa.12098

Mullen, E. M. (1997). *Mullen scales of early learning.* Los Angeles: Western Psychological Services.

Ozonoff, S., Young, G. S., Carter, A., Messinger, D., Yirmiya, N., Zwaigenbaum L., et al. (2001). Recurrence risk for autism spectrum disorders: A Baby Siblings Research Consortium study. *Pediatrics.* 128: e488-e495.

Sparrow, S. S., Cicchetti, D. V., & Balla, D. A., (2005). *Vineland adaptive behavior scales: Survey interview form/caregiver rating form* (2nd ed). (Vineland II). Livonia, MN: Pearson Assessments.

Volkmar, F. R., Chawarska, K., & Klin, A. (2008). Autism spectrum disorders in infants and toddlers. In K. Chawarska, A. Klin, & F. R. Volkmar (Eds). *Autism spectrum disorders in infants and toddlers: Diagnosis, assessment, and treatment* (pp. 1-22). New York, NY: Guilford Press.

Don't Delay! The Benefits of Early Intensive Interventions

The Fernandez Family

For several months, Enrique and Pilar Fernandez had been worried about their son, Alfredo. Shortly before Alfredo celebrated his first birthday, he had begun gradually slipping away from them, becoming more and more inaccessible and difficult to manage. For example, he would sit on the rug in his bedroom spinning the wheels of his truck with his finger and gazing at the wheel, but never rolling the truck on the floor. If Enrique tried to roll the truck on the floor, Alfredo would have a tantrum and struggle with his father to get the truck back so that he could again spin the wheels with his finger.

At their pediatrician's recommendation, Enrique and Pilar brought their now 14-month-old son to see a pediatric neurologist. She told them that Alfredo was at risk of developing an autism spectrum disorder by the time he was three years old.

Determined to get the very best care they could find for their son, the Fernandezes asked the neurologist what they could do to help their boy. She suggested trying developmentally sensitive applied behavior analysis (ABA), since the best evidence available suggested it was the most effective approach for toddlers and preschoolers. She gave them an article to read, a contact person at the state's early intervention program, and a list of websites they could check

Enrique and Pilar visited several websites to see what other parents and professionals were saying about ABA. The information was reassuring. They found a fair amount of recent research on the response of very young children to intensive early intervention in the home or in a specialized clinic. Although children varied in how much benefit they derived *from ABA treatment, almost every child made meaningful progress with these methods. Enrique and Pilar decided they would give ABA a try and see if it could be helpful for Alfredo.*

Early Intensive Behavioral Treatment

As Enrique and Pilar Fernandez realized, before you enroll your child with an ASD in a treatment program, you should be certain the program has a good, evidence-based track record of helping children maximize their potential. This chapter summarizes some of the research on treatments that have good research support to document their benefits.

Applied behavior analysis (ABA) has the best *empirically documented* effectiveness in treating children aged 3 to 5 years who have a diagnosis of an autism spectrum disorder (ASD). By "empirically documented," we mean that there is solid evidence, not just anecdotal reports, that a treatment works. A number of studies have consistently shown favorable changes in preschool-aged children who receive ABA treatment.

Briefly, ABA involves using what we know about how people learn to arrange very specific interactions with your child. For example, you might give a very specific instruction such as "give ball" and hold out your hand, and gently help her place the ball in your hand. You then provide praise and other things she likes when she is successful. That is a very simple explanation of a powerful set of teaching procedures that we describe in more detail in the next chapter.

Ivar Lovaas (1987), who was a professor in the Department of Psychology at the University of California in Los Angeles, did the earliest research on the benefits of intensive ABA treatment for preschool-aged children with autism. In his early study, he compared children receiving intensive treatment for 40 hours a week or more to two other groups of children. The group receiving intensive treatment consisted of 19 children who received 40 hours a week or more of intensive, home-based ABA for at least two years. A second group (a control group) received 10 hours or fewer of ABA treatment each week, and another control group received the standard educational services available in their California community in the mid-1980s.

The results clearly favored the intensive ABA group that received at least 40 hours of treatment a week. In this group, 47 percent of the children showed a strong, measurable, positive change following treatment. This response to treatment was reflected in their inclusion in regular education settings, where they were able to handle the academic demands of a first grade classroom. These children also showed a mean (average) 31-point increase in IQ from before to after treatment. In contrast, children in the two comparison groups made minimal IQ or educational gains over the same time span.

Importantly, all except one of the children in the intensive treatment group maintained over time the changes that they had made during treatment. In 1993, three researchers (McEachin, Smith, and Lovaas) again contacted the children who had been part of the original 1987 study to see how they were doing. At the end of the initial study, the children were about 7 years of age, and at the time of the follow-up study, they averaged 13 years. The positive news was that 8 of the 9 children with the best outcomes from the initial study were still handling the academic demands they faced at school, and also gaining age-appropriate adaptive skills. During clinical interviews, these 8 children could not be distinguished from typically developing comparison youngsters. None of the children in either control group were able to function on this level. The one child from the intensive treatment condition who did not sustain his initial progress had been removed from a regular education class and placed in a class for children who had language delays, so could no longer be said to be functioning in a "fully typical" way.

There have been a number of **systematic replications** of the initial Lovaas study. A systematic replication is one that follows most of

Table 2-1	Areas of Gain for Children in Lovaas Study

- 31-point increase in IQ (on average)
- Inclusion in regular education classroom

the same procedures of the original study, but deliberately varies some dimensions such as hours of treatment or the specific diagnosis of the children in the study. For example, one group of researchers (Smith, Groen, and Wynn, 2000) compared a program that offered 24.5 hours/ week of intensive ABA done by undergraduate treatment teams with a program in which parents were given expert training in ABA methods and asked to do about 5 hours of teaching each week. Although both conditions offered supervision and training, the children in the parent training group received many fewer hours of professional treatment. The study showed that the children who got more hours of treatment made more progress in terms of IQ, language, and academics than those in the parent training group. There were, however, no significant differences between the groups in adaptive behavior (life independence skills) or in the frequency of problem behaviors.

In another study, two researchers planned to study the benefits of an intensive treatment condition in which the children received an average of 39 hours a week of ABA treatment (Sallows and Graupner, 2005). There were two groups of children who received services provided by teams of therapists. In one group, the therapists received more professional, in-home supervision than in the other, but this did not end up having an effect on the results. Their findings were very similar to those of Lovaas: 48 percent of all the children who got intensive treatment were succeeding in regular education classes at the end of the study.

Early Intervention with Very Young Children

As discussed in Chapter 1, it is now possible to recognize the precursors of ASD in many children younger than three years of age, and it is urgent that we develop effective interventions to meet the needs of these youngsters. Because we have only recently learned to identify some of the earliest precursors of ASD, there has not been much time to do research on the treatment of infants and toddlers. As we write this book, there has only been one well-controlled study on early intervention for children under three years of age who have an ASD, or are at risk for such a diagnosis (Dawson, Rogers, Smith, Munson, Winter, et al., 2010).

Some of the most interesting work in intervention with infants and toddlers has come from psychologists Sally Rogers, Geraldine Daw-

son, and their colleagues. Their book, *Early Start Denver Model for Young Children with Autism* (Rogers & Dawson, 2010), describes their work in detail. Using the Early Start Denver Model (ESDM), Rogers and Dawson studied how to intervene with children 18 to 30 months of age who were diagnosed with an ASD or judged to be at serious risk for a diagnosis as they got older.

Using the ESDM approach, both trained professionals and parents act as primary treatment providers for an infant or toddler. The approach can also be used in a small group setting. There is a focus on creating a warm and supportive environment that encourages very young children and their parents or teachers to interact with each other.

Some Supportive Elements of the ESDM Approach

1. An attentive adult
2. Sensitivity to the child's needs
3. Using reinforcers that interest the child
4. Respecting the child's choice of activities
5. Reinforcing the child's attempts to reach a goal. It doesn't have to be perfect!
6. Back and forth shared control of activities between child and adult

---

The ESDM approach emphasizes intensive teaching in the context of play and integrating developmental, behavioral, and relationship-based approaches to treating the very young child. One of the interesting aspects of this approach is that ABA methods are used with a sensitive attunement to the development needs of the individual children. For example, the approach starts with the skills the child is able to demonstrate and builds on them.

Although sensitivity to children's interests and concerns is not unique to the ESDM model, Rogers and her colleagues are the first to clearly articulate the importance of this factor in working with young children and applying *naturalistic* methods of ABA intervention. Naturalistic teaching is different from the structured teaching used in discrete trial instruction where the adult selects the goal and creates the structure. In naturalistic teaching, adults follow the child's interest in the environment and provide multiple opportunities to explore activities. The term "naturalistic" does not mean that the adult has no goal for the session, but he or she selects items that are both of interest to the child and can be used to teach a lesson. For example, if your child likes a particular stuffed animal, you might try to teach her to enjoy trading the animal back and forth and show her some creative ways to play with it.

An essential component of the ESDM is the use of *Pivotal Response Training* (PRT) as a relaxed, comfortable way to get the child interested and engaged. Chapter 3 discusses using PRT to teach new behaviors to children with ASD. For now, it is sufficient to note that PRT is an ABA teaching method that is useful in helping children on the spectrum learn fundamental skills, including turn taking, joint attention, speech, and nonverbal exchanges between parents and children. Parents and professionals who use the ESDM also learn how to reduce a child's challenging behavior by changing their own behavior or by changing the learning context they have created for the child.

Several studies have shown that the ESDM can benefit very young children on the autism spectrum (e.g., Vismara and Rogers, 2008; Vismara, Colombi, and Rogers, 2000). The most important and rigorous empirical study was undertaken by Geraldine Dawson and her colleagues (2010). This well-designed study involved randomly assigning 48 children and their parents to different treatment conditions. Half of the children were in the ESDM program and the other half participated in other community treatments for two years. At the end of two years, the children who were treated in the ESDM showed a mean increase in Mullen Early Learning scores of 19.1 points as compared to 7 points in the comparison group. For the ESDM group, much of this improvement came from bigger gains in producing and comprehending speech (expressive and receptive language).

At the end of the study, all of the children in both groups still had a diagnosis of ASD. However, more children in the ESDM group had fewer core symptoms of ASD than children in the comparison group did. Because the children were randomly assigned to the two different conditions, these findings are especially important. They suggest the need for additional research on this new, promising approach to the treatment of very young children.

In 2012, Dawson, Rogers, and their colleagues reported additional encouraging information about the children who had been part of their randomized trial with the ESDM. Using an electroencephalograph (EEG), they measured the brainwave activity of the children from both groups of the study as well as a typically developing group of young children (The EEG is a noninvasive procedure that involves using electrodes to pick up brain activity in various parts of the brain.) The children who had been in the group receiving the ESDM treatment showed brain function similar to that of the typical children, while the children who had been in the comparison group showed an atypical pattern. This finding, although it will need to be replicated (repeated) before we can say for sure, suggests *that early intensive intervention can actually normalize the brain function of some children who receive treatment at a very early age!*

Is Recovery Possible?

One of the most urgent questions that faces professionals and parents is whether "recovery" is possible for children with ASD who receive early intensive treatment. At the time of this writing, the answer seems to be "perhaps."

The research by Geraldine Dawson described above suggests that intensive intervention that is developmentally sensitive *can* alter brain function in some very young children. But we do not yet know how much of an impact it is possible to have on the long-term developmental trajectory of children. To learn that, long term follow up of the children in Dawson's study and of other children who undergo similar treatments will be required.

Some people argue that there are adults who once had an autism spectrum diagnosis and who are now totally indistinguishable from their peers. Others, however, say that even when children make dramatic changes, there are likely to be subtle residual signs that will be evident to a well-trained professional, but perhaps not to a lay person.

A series of studies by University of Connecticut Professor of Psychology Deborah Fein and her colleagues explored the question of which children with ASD are likely to have an optimal outcome. They did an in-depth review of the research (Helt, Kelley, Kinsbourne, Pandey, Boorstein, et al., 2008) and found that there are characteristics that can predict the "best outcome." These include having a relatively high IQ (in the average range), good receptive language (language comprehension skills), the ability to imitate words and movements, and good motor development. Other positive predictors include: being young when first diagnosed, receiving early treatment, and having a diagnosis of a relatively mild ASD.

Children who have a lower probability of a "best outcome" tend to have more complex biological factors such as seizure disorders, intellectual disability (i.e., what used to be called mental retardation), or a genetic syndrome such as fragile X or Rett syndrome. However, even children who do not achieve a best outcome can still make major gains with early intensive treatment. No child should be denied this opportunity.

Table 2-2	Predictors of Best Outcome from Fein Group Study

- Good receptive language
- Verbal and motor imitation skills
- Early intervention

In their own research on children who achieved an optimal outcome, this group of investigators found that the children still had residual language deficits (Kelley, Paul, Fein, & Naigles, 2006). That is, after treatment for ASD, these children were in age appropriate classrooms, had IQs in the normal range, and were regarded as functioning about as well as the other students in the classroom. However, a close look showed that their language usage differed in subtle but important ways from their classmates'. On the positive side, the children had vocabularies comparable to their peers' and were within the norms for children their age when it came to grammar and some aspects of complex language.

In spite of their verbal strengths, these children had more difficulties than their classmates on a theory of mind task measuring the ability to understand another person's view of an event. That is, it was harder for them to put themselves in another person's shoes and imagine what he or she was thinking. Problems with theory of mind are very common in people with ASD. The children also had more trouble describing a story they had read to another person. For example, they were less likely than their peers to discuss a character's goals and motivations for behavior. They were also more likely to misinterpret the story they had read. When the children participated in the study, they were between the ages of five and nine years. It will be important to see whether they continue to make gains in these areas of language difficulty as they get older.

In a recent study, Dr. Fein and her colleagues (2013) compared 34 children and young adults who were categorized as:

1. having had a previous diagnosis of ASD, but at the time of the study having had an optimal outcome (OO),
2. having a diagnosis of high functioning autism (HFA), or
3. having no previous diagnosis of ASD and being typically developing (TD).

These three groups, matched for age and gender, were compared with one another on a number of measures. The results showed that the OO group and the TD group were very similar in their functioning, while the HFA group demonstrated significant symptoms of ASD. Simply put, the children in the optimal outcome group could not readily be discriminated from the typically developing group. However, the authors did not rule out more subtle differences between the OO and TD groups and are analyzing their data to search for such differences. If any subtle differences are found, it would be interesting, but it would not alter the good news that the optimal outcome group was functioning overall much like their typically developing peers.

We still do not know what percentage of children with ASD are able to move into the optimal outcome group. We are also still waiting for definitive data about which treatment methods led to the highest percentage of children with optimal outcomes. In the study by Dr. Fein and colleagues, most of the OO participants came from the northeastern part of the U.S. and had received behavioral treatment, although some had received other forms of intervention. It will be important for Dr. Fein's study to be replicated with children from other parts of the United States or other countries to identify variations that may occur.

Summary

There is good research showing that some young children with ASD who receive intensive ABA services during the preschool years make very good developmental gains. Some of them show an increase in IQ points and adaptive behavior and are able to do quite well in age appropriate, regular education classrooms. Other children who receive the same opportunities do not make as much progress. Still, essentially every child with ASD benefits from intensive teaching in the early years.

Progress in identifying children under age three who show early signs of having an autism spectrum disorder has lead to the development of instructional methods that help these babies and toddlers make very important progress. Many of these methods are based on principles of applied behavior analysis and will be discussed in the following chapters.

References

Dawson, G., Rogers, S. J., Smith, M., Munson, J., Winter, J., et al. (2010). Randomized controlled trial of the Early Start Denver Model: A relationship-based developmental and behavioral intervention for toddlers with autism spectrum disorders: Effects on IQ, adaptive behaviors, and autism diagnosis. *Pediatrics, 125,* 1-7.

Dawson, G., Jones, E. J. H., Merkle, K., Venema, K., Lowy, R., Faja, S., et al. (2012). Early behavioral intervention is associated with normalized brain activity in young children with autism. *Journal of the American Academy of Child & Adolescent Psychiatry, 51,* 1150-1159.

Fein, D., Barton, M., Eigsti, I., Kelley, E., Naigles, L., Schultz, R. T., & Tyson, K. (2013). Optimal outcome in individuals with a history of autism. *Journal of Child Psychology and Psychiatry, 54*(2), 195-205.

Helt, M., Kelley, E., Kinsbourne, M., Pandey, J., Boorstein, H., Herbert, M., & Fein, D. (2008). Can children with autism recover? If so, how? *Neuropsychology Review, 18*, 339-366.

Kelly, E., Paul, J. J., Fein, D., & Naigles, L. R. (2006). Residual language deficits in optimal outcome children with a history of autism. *Journal of Autism and Developmental Disorders, 36*, 807-828.

Lovaas, O. I. (1987). Behavioral treatment and normal educational and intellectual functioning in young autistic children. *Journal of Consulting and Clinical Psychology, 55*, 3-9.

McEachin, J. J., Smith, T., & Lovaas, O. I. (1993). Long-term outcome for children with autism who received early intensive behavioral treatment. *American Journal on Mental Retardation, 97*, 359-372.

Rogers, S. J., & Dawson, G. (2010). *Early Start Denver Model for Young Children with Autism: Promoting Language, Learning, and Engagement.* New York, NY: The Guilford Press.

Sallows, G. O., & Graupner, T. D. (2005). Intensive behavioral treatment for children with autism: Four-year outcome and predictors. *American Journal on Mental Retardation, 110*, 417-438.

Smith, T., Groen, A., & Wynn, J. (2000). Randomized trial of intensive early intervention for children with pervasive developmental disorder. *American Journal on Mental Retardation, 105*, 269-285.

3 | The Proven, Powerful Intervention for ASD: Applied Behavior Analysis

The Morgan Family

Aiesha and Quincy Morgan had been concerned about their son Anjou's behavior well before his first birthday. As a tiny infant, Anjou had been a cuddly little bundle and had seemed to be developing well for his first six months. After that age, Anjou gradually became fussy, no longer looked at his parents' faces very much, rarely smiled, and pushed away when they tried to cuddle him. This had happened so slowly that at first they were not sure he was really changing. But by ten months of age, Anjou was clearly very different than his older sister, Latasha, had been at that same age. She had been easy to comfort when she was upset, bounced in her crib with pure delight when they came in to pick her up after her nap, and babbled a great deal. Anjou was silent except for his screams of protest, was not interested in his parents, and was slow to recover when he got upset.

When the Morgans took Anjou to the pediatrician for his one-year well-baby checkup, they shared their concerns that their son was not interested in them, did not respond when they called his name, was almost impossible to comfort when he got upset, and could not point to any body parts. If his sister fell down and cried, he paid no attention. The pediatrician listened carefully to their concerns. As he examined Anjou, he noted that the boy did not look at him, stiffened when he was gently touched, and did not try to join in on a game of "pat-a-cake" with him.

Although the pediatrician was not certain of the diagnosis, he realized that Anjou had a number of unusual behaviors, so he made a referral to the local children's hospital, where they could do a full diagnostic evaluation. The Morgans were both upset and relieved that the doctor had understood their concerns and had given them a referral for an evaluation.

The diagnostic team did several assessments of Anjou. His parents were present during these procedures and observed how their son responded—or, more often, did not respond—to the specialists who worked with him. After the testing was over, Aiesha and Quincy met with the members of the team for feedback about Anjou's performance. The psychologist told them that Anjou was at high risk of being diagnosed with an autism spectrum disorder by the time he was three years old. She also told them they were fortunate to have recognized so early that Anjou's development was not going well and to have alerted the pediatrician to their concerns. Besides providing a package of information about autism spectrum disorders, she urged the Morgans to contact the state's early intervention services and gave them the phone number of the person they could call.

Although they were upset and frightened, the Morgans were also relieved to have something to do that might help Anjou. Within six weeks, they had enrolled him in early intervention services and were on their way to learning a new set of skills that would help them teach Anjou in a way that he could understand. They were learning to use applied behavior analysis to teach new behaviors in tiny bits that were interesting to Anjou, but not overly demanding. The emphasis was on helping him begin to value his parents and his sister as intriguing people to be with because of all the cool things they offered him. Anjou's parents and teachers also increased the predictable routines in his life so that he would anticipate what was happening next throughout the day and develop a sense of order. Thanks to early intervention, ABA, and their increased sensitivity to Anjou, Aiesha and Quincy were helping their son become part of the family.

How Do We Learn?

We are born with some "hardwired' behaviors in our brains that enable us to survive the earliest months of our lives. As babies, we reflexively know how to suck to get food from our mother's breast or a bottle, we draw away from things that hurt us, we cry when we are in distress, and we find people's faces especially interesting. Without these abilities, humans as we know them would long ago have vanished from the earth. But we need many more adaptive behaviors in order to grow into social, communicating people who are part of the culture that surrounds us. We learn those skills through our own observations of the world, from instructions of our parents, siblings, and teachers, from what we see on television and computer screens, and, as we learn to read, from the written word.

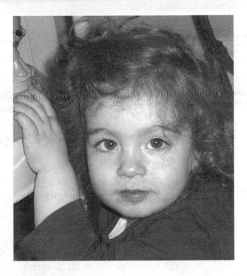

To develop the skills in communication, social interaction, problem solving, and self-care that are so vital to our ability to function well with our family, our peers, and our wider culture, we need to be able to learn from other people. Fortunately, our brains have evolved over eons so that there are areas of the brain that can learn these skills and enable us to speak, experience emotion, remember events, and so forth. For typically developing infants, much of the earliest learning is acquired through contact with parents and other nurturing adults and through the brain's ability to seek patterns in the environment.

Because babies need adults in order to obtain food, dry diapers, help in falling asleep, and gentle, playful stimulation, parents are a powerful source of reinforcement (reward) for infants. Infants study their parents' faces, track their eye movements, and gradually acquire what we call *joint attention.* Joint attention refers to the ability of two people to both gaze at an object or activity and to look at one another to share their mutual awareness. When two tourists stand at the Grand Canyon, look down to the bottom, and then glance at one another, that is a moment of joint attention and communication through gaze, and, perhaps, a spoken "wow." Joint attention also occurs when an adult and child focus on the same object and the parent names the object— for example, "cup." This type of interaction helps the child begin to recognize that familiar objects have names. Ultimately, he learns to say these names to label and request them.

Up to the age of about six months, most babies who are at risk of being diagnosed with an ASD do not appear much different from their neurotypical peers. After that age, no matter how attentive his parents are, the toddler who has ASD does not usually engage in much, if any, joint attention. This failure makes learning the names of objects and actions much more difficult, as the child may be looking at the ceiling one time and at his mother's shoulder another time when she is naming a "cup." As a result, he is much less likely to pick up a useful vocabulary of basic names.

The brain deficits in children with ASD also make the process of *attachment* to parents more difficult. The term "attachment" refers to the emotional bond that a baby forms with his mother and father. The tender care his parents provide makes them very powerful sources of reward and they are the infant's first "love." A typically developing infant or toddler looks to his parents for reassurance and help when he is afraid or upset. In contrast, a child with ASD does not seek comfort from his parents' eyes or face.

Failing to read the social cues that typical children recognize when interacting with their parents puts children with ASD at a major social and linguistic disadvantage. Because of these biologically based deficits, it is urgent that we teach children with ASD the skills that will help them relate to caring adults in more typical ways.

Fortunately, it is possible for trained professionals to teach joint attention and symbolic play in fairly brief sessions that help children become more aware of others and develop a broader range of play skills (e.g., Goods, Ishijima, Chang, and Kasari, 2012). The very good news is that recent research suggests that parents can also teach their children joint attention skills. In a study with toddlers who were at risk for ASD and their parents, half of the toddlers and parents were randomly assigned to receive immediate training in the procedures and half were in a wait-list control group. The children in the immediate treatment group made rapid gains. Even a year later, they were still responding better to adult bids for joint attention and had more functional skills than the children in the wait list control group (Kasari, Gulsrud, Wong, Kwon, and Locke, 2010). They did not, however, try to initiate joint attention with another person more often than the children in the control group. In another study, one of the authors of this book and a colleague found that it was possible to train 6- to 8-year-old siblings of children on the autism spectrum how to teach their brother or sister to establish joint attention with them (Ferraioli and Harris, 2011).

About ABA

As we described in Chapter 2, the treatment methods for ASD with the most research support are based on the principles of applied behavior analysis (ABA). The term applied behavior analysis refers to the notion that by closely studying (analyzing) how to teach new skills (behaviors), we can make it easier for a person to master those skills. Through ABA, it is possible to match our teaching methods to the needs of the student.

There is a great deal of research showing that parents and teachers can learn ABA methods and apply them effectively at home, in the community, and in the classroom. The best way to learn the ABA techniques is to have someone who understands how to use these methods show you what to do. That might be your child's teacher or a Board Certified Behavior Analyst who works with your child in your home, or you might attend a series of classes offered by an autism advocacy group in your state. Some people find that grasping the principles behind ABA instructional methods helps them organize their thinking about ABA and decide when to use the different methods.

In this chapter we will link the ways that children learn through the ABA procedures that can facilitate learning. This chapter is a primer on ABA that will introduce you to some of the basic concepts. We will discuss some of the fundamentals, with an emphasis on teaching in *naturalistic settings,* because that is where so much effective teaching with infants, toddlers, and young children occurs. By "naturalistic" we mean the types of relatively unstructured playful interactions that parents offer all of their children, whether or not they have a disability. For example, sitting on your child's bedroom floor and rolling a ball back and forth with him or talking with him as you help him dress or take a bath are all natural interactions that can provide learning opportunities.

The many strategies of ABA can be used in naturalistic settings as well as in more structured *discrete trial instruction* (DTI). DTI involves an adult-controlled interaction in which the teacher or parent gives the child an instruction (e.g., "Point to book"), and the child is expected to point to that object. We will discuss naturalistic teaching in more depth than DTI because it is used more widely with very young children.

Table 3-1	ABA Teaching Vocabulary

- Baseline Data (see page 40)
- Chaining (see page 45)
- Discrete Trial Instruction (DTI) (see page 46)
- Functional Behavior Assessment (FBA) (see page 40)
- Functional Behavior Analysis (see page 41)
- Gestural Prompts (see page 44)
- Physical Prompts (see page 44)
- Pivotal Response Training (PRT) (see page 42)
- Position Prompts (see page 45)
- Reinforcement (see page 38)
- Shaping (see page 45)

Reinforcement

The focus of this book is not on the comprehensive use of ABA to teach your child new skills, but there is some basic terminology that will be helpful to you. One of the most important instructional methods in the ABA toolbox is the use of *reinforcement* or rewards.

For parents of young children without autism spectrum disorders, it is usually pretty easy to figure out what motivates their children to learn. Often it is attention from the parents themselves—smiles, goofy faces, tickles, gentle roughhousing—or words of praise. Because infants and toddlers with ASD initially may not understand or care about their parents' gestures or words, we have to closely observe them to figure out

what motivates them. That is, what items or activities are an incentive for them to attend to and participate with the adult?

Once you know what motivates your child, you can provide him with that item or experience (reinforce him) when he does his best to respond to your requests. By reinforcing his behavior, you make it more likely that he will follow your requests in the future.

One of the important concepts underlying ABA is the use of reinforcement to establish and maintain behavior. You are going to ask your child to do things that are not always easy for him. You will want to be able to motivate him to try his best to learn a new skill.

In order to get your child to work hard at learning, you need to identify things that he is willing to work for. You may, for example, know that your child loves vanilla ice cream more than any other food. You might offer him small tastes of that ice cream when he tries to do something that you are teaching him. For example, if you want him to imitate you when you pretend to feed a doll, you could say something like, "One for the baby," and pause while he offers the doll a bite of play food. They you might say, "And one for you. Great job feeding your doll." And then give him a small spoon of vanilla ice cream along with your praise. If your child loves to be spun in the air you might want to teach him to say "spin" and then reinforce him by picking him up, saying "great talking," and spinning him around the room.

For many children with ASD, it is relatively easy to identify activities, foods, and objects that are attractive enough to motive them to play with adults and follow simple requests. There are some children who are not as easily motivated, however, and we have written a book in the Woodbine House autism series about how to motivate these more reluctant learners (Delmolino & Harris, 2004).

It helps if your child finds several different items or experiences to be motivating. You can let your child select the thing he wants or offer him different choices for different activities. Most of us like to have choices.

Some parents have asked whether providing reinforcement is bribing their child to do something that the child should want do. The term "bribery" implies asking people to violate their own values and to do things that are "wrong." Offering praise and access to a desirable experience is not bribery—it is creating motivation for a child who is working hard to learn a skill.

Neither is offering your child a toss in the air or a piece of a chocolate chip cookie treating him like a "pet." Pets do respond to incentives to learn new skills such as putting out a paw to "shake hands." But, your goals for your child are not to teach him a few "tricks," but to teach him the essential skills he needs to become aware of other people and of himself and to enjoy the possibilities of his life.

Data

Throughout this book we mention the importance of collecting data on your child's performance of skills you are teaching him. ABA is a data-driven teaching method. That is, people using ABA rely on objective data about events that can be observed when determining whether a teaching approach is working, rather than trusting subjective impressions. If an approach is effective, they continue using it. But if an approach is not benefitting the child, they change it. Your child's early learning years are too precious to waste on ineffective programs!

With all of the programs for children with ASD at the Douglass Developmental Disabilities Center, we begin by collecting baseline data to determine whether or not the child already has the skill we plan to teach. *Baseline data* show what a person is doing or how he is functioning before some kind of intervention or treatment is tried.

When using ABA strategies with your child, you will need to first obtain baseline data to determine how often or how well he does a particular behavior. For example, if you wanted to teach your child to imitate your behaviors, you might start by saying "Do this" and stack one block on top of another. If your child ignored you, or followed the instruction only once in a while, you would have a very low "baseline" performance. Then, you would teach your child how to stack the blocks and keep track of the number of times he imitated you after you gave the instruction to "Do this." This way you could objectively evaluate how well your teaching procedures were working. However, if your child imitated you consistently during the baseline phase when you were not actively teaching him to imitate, you would know that he already had that necessary skill. If so, you could devote your time to working on other useful skills.

Functional Behavior Assessment

It is useful to collect baseline data both for skills you want to increase and for inappropriate behaviors that you want to decrease. In the case of an inappropriate behavior such as tantrums, your goal would be to decrease the frequency of the behavior.

Sometimes if a behavior is especially problematic, you may need to have a teacher or behavior analyst do a *functional behavior assessment* to determine the specific situations in which your child has tantrums. The behavior analyst can then help you come up with a program that allows your child to receive reinforcement without resorting to tantrums. This process might start with the analyst asking you whether there seem to be specific conditions that trigger tantrums or other behavior. For example, you might have observed that your child is more likely to have a tantrum when you try to join in his use of toy cars. You might then be asked to collect some data on when the tantrums are occurring.

Sometimes when the function is not clear, it is necessary to do a *functional behavior analysis.* This is a subcategory of a functional behavior assessment in which we actively manipulate different events that might result in tantrums. That is, the home consultant or behavior analyst systematically introduces various conditions to see how they affect your child's behavior. These conditions can include an "alone" condition during which your child is allowed to do whatever he wishes. In a "demand" condition, your child is asked to comply with instructions from the adult. The purpose of a functional behavior analysis is to determine what function the tantrum serves for your child. For example, does it allow him to escape from your current request? Does it allow him to gain your attention? What occurs as a result of the tantrum that is reinforcing to your child?

Once it is clear what function the behavior is serving, you and the behavior analyst or consultant can find a way to address the behavior. For example, if your child uses tantrums to avoid work, he might be taught to use a hand gesture or a picture to tell you he doesn't want to do what you requested. Once he can do that rather than tantrum, you can gradually introduce small requests and richly reinforce him for cooperation. Over time, you can make more requests and trim back the magnitude of the rewards.

Creating the Right Context for Learning

Typically developing infants and toddlers learn best when they are emotionally engaged with the people and things around them (Rogers & Dawson, 2010). It is not just hearing speech that teaches children to talk. The littlest learners also need to hear words in a warm social context with parents who talk about the world and make playful gestures, funny sounds, cuddles, and laughable faces that are attuned to their child's mood in the moment. It is also essential that parents know when to cut back on stimulation as well as when to intensify it. These interactions help infants or toddlers to gradually make sense of their world as they recognize patterns that recur over time.

Because some brain functions of children with ASDs are different than those of typically developing children, infants and toddlers with ASD may not find it rewarding to interact with their parents at first. Like Anjou, some young children with ASD stiffen and cry when touched; others do not pay attention to the person who holds them. As a result, parents, teachers, and others have to go about teaching children with ASD much more systematically, ensuring that they create situations that are interesting and attractive. As adults in your child's life pair themselves with rewarding events, they will become more reinforcing for your child.

Chapter 7 describes several ways to enhance the pleasure your child gets from being with you, such as tossing him in the air. Over time, your child will be willing to tolerate short delays before he gains access to the pleasures you have to offer. Those delays give you opportunities to make small requests of your child. For example, if he is waiting for you to swing him in the air, you can ask him to first imitate putting his hands up. Then, when he does, you can pick him up and give him a swing.

Pivotal Response Training

One useful package of ABA techniques is called **Pivotal Response Training** (PRT). This approach was developed by Robert and Lynn Koegel and by Laura Schreibman and her colleagues as a way to teach some of the important basic skills that children with ASD need to learn. PRT address an array of fundamental skills such as increasing a child's motivation to respond to adult requests, as well as his ability to recognize and use cues in the environment to understand what behavior is called for. These skills are "pivotal" because they are useful in multiple settings with multiple skills.

A good example of using a PRT technique to increase a baby's attempts to communicate appears in a recent pilot study (Steiner, Gengoux, Klin, and Chawarska, 2013). These authors taught the parents of three babies at risk for ASD to use Pivotal Response training to increase their children's motivation to try to communicate with them. The children were all "baby sibs" of older brothers or sisters who were diagnosed with ASD. During the baseline assessment, all three babies made very few attempts to communicate. But after their parents started using PRT methods, the babies all made many more responses. Some of the strategies the parents learned included responding to their children's choice of interesting things to look at, reinforcing their children's attempts to communicate their interests, and rewarding their children often with naturalistic reinforcers such as cuddles and tickles. After the introduction of this treatment, the authors reported a clear increase in the babies' attempts to communicate with their parents.

To motivate very young children with ASD to engage with us, we need to figure out which experiences seem most interesting to the children and then make those available. At our Center, we do a lot of teaching of very young children in natural settings. We first create a rich environment with toys and activities that may be attractive to the child. As we learn what attracts his interest the most, we can then engage him by using items and activities that he finds intriguing. When the child expresses an interest in a toy or activity, we weave our responses together with his. For example, as described below, we might insert an act of our own such as rolling a ball toward the child and then holding out our hand to receive the ball back. This way we share control over the activities with the child.

Finding things your child wants to do is part of the challenge of effective teaching. Being fully engaged with him and keeping some adult control over the activities or objects are other important components. We want a child who isn't using speech (preverbal) to learn to engage in a back-and-forth rhythm that will be the template for conversation at a later stage. For example, your child might point toward a ball and make a sound. You respond, "You want ball." You then say, "Your turn," as you hand the ball to your child. After he holds the ball, you say, "My turn." You hold it very briefly and give it back to him, saying, "Your turn."

These interactions are very busy. They require the adult's full attention so that she can judge the child's level of interest, whether his interest is shifting to other items or games, and whether the pace is too fast, too slow, or just right at that moment in time. You will learn to develop routines with your child and then gradually expand and vary the routines so your child learns to be flexible in his responses.

Prompts

Another fundamental skill for teaching very young children is the use of *physical or gestural prompts.* A prompt is a form of guidance that helps your child respond to your request.

For example, if you want your child to hand you a toy truck, you might say "give truck" and hold out your hand. If you are using a full physical prompt, you would use your other hand to put your child's hand on the truck and guide him to put the truck in your open hand. You would then reinforce him for doing as you asked. Ideally, that reinforcement would involve the truck in some interesting way. For example, you might say "Zoom, Zoom" and roll the truck on the floor as you push it toward him.

It is very important to keep your child from becoming dependent on full physical prompts. So after a few successful fully prompted trials, you could say, "Give truck" and point at the truck to see if a pointing gesture is enough for him to understand that you want the truck. If he does not respond to your point, you might lightly place your hand on the back of his hand and gently guide him toward the truck. If he still does not pick it up, you may need to give him a few more trials with a fuller prompt. Again, if you can, after he hands you the truck, use that vehicle as part of your playful reinforcement sequence. You can use

---

Examples of Prompts

Full Physical Prompt: Hand-over-hand guidance to help your child do something

Partial Physical Prompt: Gradually reducing physical assistance in completing an action (hovering your hand over your child's hand but not touching it, or sliding your hand back so you touch the wrist, forearm, and if needed, upper arm, rather than hand)

Gestural Prompt: Using a gesture to show what to do (e.g., pointing at the object to be used, or holding out your hand to receive the object)

Visual Prompt: Positioning items or using a visual reminder to help cue your child what to do (e.g., placing one of two or more objects closer to the child so he sees it first and can easily reach it)

trucks, dolls, blocks, action figures, drums, teddy bears, and other items that interest your child in this fashion.

One word of caution: When starting to teach your child to share with you, do not start with his most beloved object. Select something that he likes, but can surrender for a brief moment without a fuss.

You can also use the *position* of the object as a visual prompt for your child. For example, if you want him to select the teddy bear from

several possible objects to give you, put the bear closer to him and the truck and the ball a little farther away. That way it is easier for him to recognize the bear and give it to you. Over time, you can gradually move the three toys closer together so that he has to pay attention to all three items and select the correct one.

Other Teaching Methods

Shaping. *Shaping* is another ABA skill you can use to teach your child. It involves gradually helping your child perform a skill more and more expertly. For example, if you are teaching him to say the word "ball," you would first accept and reinforce just the "b" sound. Then you would reinforce "baa," and finally "ball" or a close approximation of the full word.

Chaining. *Chaining* is an ABA procedure in which you link together a series of steps to gradually enable a child to complete a full routine. For example, you might use chaining to teach your child to brush his teeth independently. You might start by doing all of the steps for him except rinsing his mouth at the end, and begin by teaching him to rinse on his own. You would then reinforce him for doing that final step. When he has learned to do the last step, you would have him do the next-to-last step and the last step on his own, then the one before

that, and so forth, until the whole chain is in place. When that is accomplished, you have taught your child all of the steps of the rather complex process of brushing his own teeth. See Chapter 8 for more of an overview of teaching self-help skills to your young child.

Discrete Trial Instruction. As mentioned previously, ABA strategies can be used in naturalistic settings as well as in more structured *discrete trial instruction* (DTI). In contrast to naturalistic instruction, in which instruction is designed around interests and activities the child enjoys, DTI involves adult-controlled interactions. The teacher or parent selects the instructional setting, materials, and goal. She then gives the child an instruction (e.g., "show me your nose"), and the child is expected to follow the instruction. For very young children in early intervention, an instruction would not be repeated multiple times in a row. Instead, repetitions might be woven into an interaction with his mother or father.

When teaching children using DTI, it is common to alternate previously learned material with new material. Even with older children, it is important to mix together activities or skills the children have already mastered with new skills they are learning. The technical term for this mixing of new and old is "interspersal."

Reinforcement, appropriate prompts, shaping, and chaining can all be used during DTI as well as in naturalistic, child controlled settings. However, for most young children the focus will be on naturalistic teaching. If your child needs to learn a name of an item, the name might be woven into a lesson, but would not be a "drill." After kindergarten age, children with ASD may have more encounters with DTI, as it can be an efficient way to create more intensive learning opportunities and often is compatible with learning early preschool skills. If your child's teacher or home consultant thinks that some DTI instruction might be helpful for your child, you can ask him or her to explain why and what that instruction would entail.

Be Skeptical

We use the principles of ABA in our own program at Rutgers University in New Brunswick, New Jersey. The center serves children from toddlers to adolescents up to age 21, as well as adults. We use ABA because of the large body of research that has demonstrated the power of these techniques in making a meaningful impact on the behavior of people with ASD of any age, including very young children.

Although ABA is an effective treatment for ASD, it takes training to do it correctly. If someone says he or she uses ABA, but does not collect data on your child's skill acquisition, be skeptical of the depth of the person's knowledge of ABA. Likewise be skeptical if the person does not make a meaningful attempt to analyze the roots of your child's behavior problems. Sadly, many people offer "treatments" that are not based on well-controlled studies, and others try to hitch their wagon to the ABA star, but lack deep knowledge of how to apply the principles of ABA. Consulting a Board Certified Behavior Analyst who has knowledge both of the theory of ABA and techniques for application of the theory is your best bet. Some Board Certified Behavior Analysts provide direct services, while others supervise people who are trained in how to implement these methods, but require ongoing supervision by a BCBA.

Besides learning about treatments that have been proven effective, it is also very important for you to be aware of treatments that have not been proven to work. There are some widely promoted methods that have little, if any, evidence of benefit, and there are a few methods that have the potential to be harmful. One good place to check out potentially problematic treatments is on the website of the Autism Science Foundation. Their article "Beware of Non-Evidence

Based Treatments" on that website is a good one to read. The link is: *www.autismsciencefoundation.org/what-is-autism/autism-diagnosis/ beware-non-evidence-based-treatments*.

The Autism Science Foundation website focuses on group design studies and explains the importance of this research design. Another valuable contribution to understanding the benefits of applied behavior analysis for treating ASD is found in well done "single subject" designs. A good place to go for information on single subject design and the latest research is operated by the Association for Science in Autism Treatment. Their website can be found at: www.asatonline.org.

Testimonials are not data. If someone promises you major gains and has no scientific articles to support those claims, be very skeptical of the services. Other warning flags are when people who advocate a particular treatment say their method cannot be studied or when no one has been able to replicate (repeat) the findings of the founder of the treatment.

Summary

It is important that parents and other caretakers understand the basics of ABA and know how and when to use those methods in a way that respects their child's current developmental abilities. ABA techniques have been proven to be very helpful in teaching new skills to people with ASD of all ages, including infants and toddlers. ABA methods are especially effective for helping children on the autism spectrum learn the complex skills they need to master. For very young children, these skills include the back-and-forth exchange of objects and speech with adults and peers, as well as self-help, communication, and social skills.

References

Delmolino, L., & Harris, S. L. (2004). *Incentives for change: Motivating people with autism spectrum disorders to learn and gain independence.* Bethesda, MD: Woodbine House.

Ferraioli, S. J., & Harris, S. L. (2011). Teaching joint attention to children with autism through sibling-mediated behavioral intervention. *Behavioral Interventions, 26,* 261-281.

Goods, K. S., Ishijima, E., Chang, Y., & Kasari, C. (In press). Preschool based JAS-PER intervention in minimally verbal children with autism: Pilot RCT. *Journal of Autism and Developmental Disorders.* doi: 10.1007/s10803-012-1644-3.

Kasari, C., Gulsrud, A. C., Wong, C., Kwon, S., & Locke, J. (2010). Randomized controlled caregiver mediated joint engagement intervention for toddlers with autism. *Journal of Autism and Developmental Disorders, 40,* 1045-1056.

Koegel, R. L., & Koegel, L. K. (1988). Generalized responsivity and pivotal behavior. In R. H. Horner, G. Dunlap, & R. L. Koegel (Eds.), *Generalization and maintenance: Lifestyle changes in applied settings* (pp. 41-66). Baltimore, MD: Paul H. Brookes.

Rogers, S. J., & Dawson, G. (2010). *Early Start Denver Model for young children with autism: Promoting language, learning, and engagement.* New York, NY: Guilford.

Schreibman, L., & Koegel, R. L. (2005). Training for parents of children with autism: Pivotal responses, generalization, and individualization of interventions. In E. D. Hibbs & P. S. Jensen (Eds.), *Psychosocial treatment for child and adolescent disorders: Empirically based strategies for clinical practice* (2nd ed., pp. 605-631). Washington, DC: American Psychological Association.

Steiner, A. M., Gengoux, G. W., Klin, A., & Chawarska, K. (2013). Pivotal Response treatment for infants at-risk for autism spectrum disorders: A pilot study. *Journal of Autism and Development Disorders, 43,* 91-102.

4 | Getting Your Child Ready for School:
It's Not Too Early to Start

The Chin Family

Ming and Jin Chin recognized that their youngest child, Chang, was developing in a very different way than his sister, Chun. Ming, who had an advanced degree in genetics, realized that Chang might have the symptoms of an autism spectrum disorder. She called her mentor from graduate school and asked where to take Chang for a diagnosis. The Midwestern university medical center near the Chins' home had a special program for the early identification of babies, toddlers, and preschool-aged children who might be on the spectrum. That program also provided diagnostic services, as well as center-based and home-based treatment for the children and their families.

Ming and Jin's concerns were validated by the diagnostic team who evaluated Chang. Although it was upsetting to have their fears confirmed, they were also relieved to have a clear course of action for Chang. The team that did the evaluation told them that their early intervention programs would have an opening for a toddler within six weeks and that Chang was a good candidate for that slot.

The team members also explained how important it was for Ming and Jin to be part of the treatment team, working with him at home using the same methods as the professionals who would be providing services. Since Jin worked from home most days, the Chins decided it would be simplest for him to adapt his schedule to stay with his son during the day. Ming, who worked outside of the home, would spend time teaching her son new skills later in the afternoon and on weekends. The Chins also talked at length with each other about how to make sure that their daughter, Chun, got her fair share of parent attention.

Introduction

Making sure that Chang got the services he needed was stressful for Ming and Jin. It wasn't easy for Jin to do the work he had to do each day and still make time for Chang's ABA lessons. Because Chang was just 18 months old, these lessons had to be adapted to meet his developmental needs, and both Ming and Jin had to be taught how to engage their son in interactions targeted to his toddler needs. The Chins were lucky because they had good medical insurance and Jin's

 work hours were flexible. The insurance enabled them to hire a Board Certified Behavior Analyst who was experienced in teaching very young children. This analyst worked with Chang for 10 hours a week and taught them how to work with their son. Not every family has the Chins' flexibility or insurance, and sometimes one parent has to stop working in order to participate in the child's treatment.

As a parent, you want the very best for your child and undoubtedly intend to do all you can to address the challenges that result from having an autism spectrum disorder (ASD). Some families supplement the intervention services from the public sector by hiring trained professionals to work with their child at home. Unfortunately, most of us cannot afford private services without either good insurance coverage or considerable personal wealth, but it is one way to provide a child with an ASD very intense intervention.

Families who have less money and limited or no insurance covering the treatment of autism spectrum disorders rely exclusively on publically funded early intervention services, and supplement that by working at home with their child. Once the child is preschool aged or older, many families enroll their child in a public school setting or in a home-based program funded by their local school district. Some families who have their child in a part-time public school program may continue to provide home-based services by hiring professionals and/ or working with their child themselves.

This chapter will give you an overview of the public sector services that are available for young children with autism spectrum disorders in the United States. The next chapter will focus on things you can do yourself at home and in the community to help your child learn.

Early Intervention Programs

In the United States, children under the age of three years are eligible for early intervention services. How many hours of service and what kinds of services are available vary from state to state, however, and you may have to advocate vigorously to get as many hours of service for your child as possible. Early intervention (EI) services are provided for children with many kinds of early challenges, including difficulties with motor development, cognitive development, communication skills, social/emotional development, and adaptive skills. For example, early intervention is available for infants and toddlers who have vision or hearing problems, motor or coordination problems, and intellectual disabilities.

Because ASD has an impact on multiple developmental areas, your child needs a curriculum that addresses her complex needs. You will want to be certain that the services she receives are targeted appropriately to her needs and not broadly generic in nature. Just as the Chin family did, you should also make sure that the people who work with your child are experienced in meeting the needs of young children with autism spectrum disorders.

Early intervention services are provided under Part C of the Individuals with Disabilities Education Act (IDEA)—the federal law that establishes how special education and other needed services are provided to children with disabilities aged 21 and under. Part C of this law concerns how states deliver services to children under the age of three years. When children reach three years of age, the responsibility for their services shifts to the state's educational system, and those services are provided under Part B of IDEA. If you want details on how the legislation works, you can do a computer search for "IDEA Part C" or "IDEA Part B" to get a full picture of your child's entitlements. At the end of this chapter, we have listed a couple of the many, many websites that are available to you.

Eligibility

Under the provisions of Part C of IDEA, infants and toddlers with disabilities or delays must be found *eligible* before they can receive EI services such as physical therapy, education, and support for the child and family. Under IDEA, children who may require EI or special educa-

tion services are supposed to be identified through a program called Child Find. The Child Find program is intended to increase public awareness, identify children who may be at risk, and determine their needs.

If you are concerned that your child may have ASD, you can contact the Child Find program in your area yourself. Your child's pediatrician should have the number to call for your local early intervention program. You can also check the NECTAC website listed in the Resources at the end of this chapter for the early intervention coordinator in your state. Once you contact the early intervention program, they will set up a time to assess your child to see if your concerns are warranted.

IDEA provides for an initial assessment process to determine whether your child is eligible for services. Children are generally found eligible if they are determined to have a diagnosis that is likely to cause a developmental delay in one or more areas. The goal of EI is to diminish the impact of these developmental challenges and help the child gain skills so she can learn with her same-age peers.

The evaluation and assessment process is done without charge to families. You may be asked to bring your child to a center to be assessed, or the professionals may come to your home. Professionals with expertise in all areas of suspected delay will administer tests and observe your child. They will compare her abilities with the skills that typically developing children of the same age are expected to have.

For example, a speech-language pathologist may assess your child's communication skills, and a physical or occupational therapist may assess her motor (movement) skills.

Once the evaluation is completed, you will be told whether your child qualifies for early intervention services. Your child will be eligible if she is diagnosed with a qualifying disability such as an autism spectrum disorder or a speech and language disorder, or if she is found to be sufficiently delayed in one or more developmental areas. Eligibility criteria vary from locale to locale, so speak with the early intervention professionals who evaluated your child if you have questions.

Individualized Treatment Plan (IFSP)

Once your child's evaluation is completed, a document called an *Individualized Family Service Plan (IFSP)* is created as a guide to treatment. The team that develops the IFSP includes you, the parents, as well as service providers. You will all combine your knowledge to develop a useful plan for your child and family. Parents have an important voice in this process and you should be prepared to be active participants in reviewing the plan and making requests of your own.

Your child's IFSP will include information about goals and objectives for your child and family; the services she will receive to help her meet these goals and who will provide them; and where your child will receive her instruction, therapies, and support.

Goals and Objectives. Goals address the big picture of what your child is expected to achieve. For example, a goal might be for your child to be toilet trained. Objectives break the big goal down into smaller steps. For example, objectives that your child might be expected to meet in order to achieve the previous goal include: pulling her pants down; sitting on the toilet for a few minutes; and asking verbally or through another communication system to use the toilet.

Services. The IFSP will specify what services will be provided to help your child and your family reach her goals. These might include the services of a Board Certified Behavior Analyst, an early intervention specialist, an occupational therapist, a speech-language pathologist, and other appropriate professionals. EI is also supposed to support families in their attempts to help their children, so services such as parent training and support might also be provided for you.

Every state is required to offer EI services to eligible children with disabilities from birth through 36 months. Annual funding is provided in part by funds from the federal government based on census figures. In some communities, all early intervention services are provided free of charge, regardless of the family's income level. In other communities, there is a sliding fee scale for parents who enroll their child in EI services.

Setting. The IFSP will state where your child will receive her early intervention services—in your home, in a daycare or preschool setting, in a hospital, or in a clinical center—and how often. With very few exceptions, EI services are provided in the child's home or in a community setting such as your child's daycare program or preschool. This is because IDEA emphasizes serving very young children in the child's natural environment and where typical peers might also be found. Exceptions are made only when the treatment provider and family can justify working in a more restricted setting such as a clinic or hospital.

Educational Services for Children 3 to 5 Years of Age

When your child is approaching three years of age, you and her EI team will plan for her to make the transition out of early intervention and into the educational system. This will require you to meet with a new group of service providers and work with them to develop your child's first Individualized Education Program (IEP).

Eligibility: Under IDEA regulations, preschool-aged children with an ASD are eligible for special educational services. Different states use different terms to label young children who are eligible for preschool programs. The majority of states identify these children as having "developmental delay" or "significant developmental delay." If the child has another diagnostic label such as autism spectrum disorder, some states will use that diagnosis.

As with early intervention, there is a process that children need to go through to establish their eligibility for preschool services. (This is also true for special education services in elementary school.) Your child will be evaluated by a team of specialists to determine whether she has delays or a disability that will have an educational impact on her. Again, this evaluation will be completed at no cost to you.

If your child has been receiving EI services, the EI team will arrange the evaluation for you. If your child is between 3 and 5 and has not previously received services, you can refer her for the evaluation yourself. The special education department at your local elementary school should be able to tell you whom to contact to begin the process.

IEP: If your child qualifies for preschool (or elementary school) services, you will meet with a team of professionals to develop an Individualized Education Program (IEP). An IEP is similar to an IFSP, but the focus is solely on the child's need, rather than on both the child's and family's needs.

Like IFSPs, IEPs include goals that describe what your child's team (including you, the parent) would like to see her achieve. These goals are based on your child's "present level of performance," as revealed by testing and observation of your child. For example, your three-year-old might be found to be using speech at the level of a child who is 24 months old. If so, an overall goal might be for her to acquire more age appropriate speech.

The IEP will specify what services will be provided to help your child meet her goals. These may include speech-language therapy, occupational or physical therapy, and assistance in acquiring social and play skills. The IEP will also include information on how often the services will be provided. For example, your child might have three half-hour sessions with the speech-language pathologist every week to support her learning more advanced speech.

Setting: Your child's IEP team is not supposed to decide on the setting where your child will receive her services until her goals have been agreed upon. Some children are placed in classes with typically developing children and others are placed in classes that focus on children with disabilities. Based on the IEP, services for preschool-aged children can include full- or half-day preschool classes, and an extended school year of 12 months.

Your child should be placed in the setting that her IEP team determines is the *"least restrictive environment"* where she can accomplish her goals. Under IDEA, the LRE is the setting in which a child is able to have the maximum amount of contact with typically developing peers while still making appropriate progress on her goals. So, if the team thinks a child can make good progress in a regular education classroom with instruction from a general education teacher, that is the LRE for her. If the team believes that she needs a quieter environment, more intensive or specialized instruction, or focused attention to diminish problem behaviors such as aggressive or self-injurious behavior, then the LRE for her might be a special education classroom. Some children might split their time between a regular education and special education classroom.

Home based instruction may also be available for children who require that intensity of teaching. But in many states, the number of hours of home based services is short of the 20 to 25 hours that is widely regarded as the *minimum* for effective treatment for autism spectrum disorders. It then falls to the parents to provide those additional hours themselves or by hiring an outside consultant.

Transition to Kindergarten: When your child ages out of preschool special education and is eligible for kindergarten, another educational team meeting is involved to create a new IEP appropriate for the school-aged youngster. Ages of eligibility for kindergarten vary from state to state. In some states, children remain eligible for preschool services until they turn six. In others, eligibility for preschool services ends on a certain date—such as August 31ˢᵗ—in the year they turn five.

The IEP written for your child's kindergarten year will have more emphasis on academics than her preschool IEPs did. However, goals can still be written for other areas that affect your child's ability to function successfully at school. For example, your child's IEP team might decide it is important to focus on specific social and self-help skills that will help her cope with the demands of kindergarten. Your child can also continue to receive speech-language, occupational, or other therapies. In addition, the IEP team may recommend including a behavior management plan in the IEP, if there are concerns that your child may engage in challenging behaviors.

Your Role on the IEP Team

As a parent, you must be given the opportunity to be involved in this IEP decision-making process. You will get written notices when your child is identified as needing services, when she is evaluated, and when a placement is going to be determined. You will be invited to every IEP meeting, and if the date selected does not fit your schedule, you can ask the school to choose another date.

It is a good idea to prepare for IEP meetings in advance. That is, spend some time thinking about what *you* would most like to see your child learn to do (or not do). Then come prepared to advocate for the goals you would like your child to reach, as well as the services that you believe would help her reach those goals. It can also be very helpful to come prepared to share specific examples of what does and does not help your child learn and follow behavioral expectations. Feel free also to share insights into her special interests and talents that might not be apparent from the evaluation.

Unfortunately, although IDEA requires that an *individualized education program* be developed for each child with a disability, it does not require that schools provide the *best* possible program for each child. Instead, IDEA requires that children be given an *appropriate* education. (Courts have interpreted this as meaning a program that provides "some benefit" to the child.) Not surprisingly, parents and school personnel sometimes disagree about what is and is not appropriate for any given child with ASD.

You cannot be compelled to sign an IEP if you do not agree with it. If it is your child's first IEP, the school cannot even implement the IEP without your signature. However, for subsequent IEPs, many states allow the school to proceed with implementing an IEP over a parent's objections.

If you disagree with actions taken by your child's school, you can ask for a meeting with the IEP team. You can bring a friend, an advocate, or a lawyer to the meeting to help you argue for what you think is right. If you are still not satisfied, you can request a mediation process. Ultimately, if you do not believe the IEP proposed is in the best interests of your child, you can request an impartial hearing. Before taking such drastic measures, however, it is often better to work collaboratively with your IEP team and try to reach a compromise.

Summary

Thanks to research on the very early identification of children who are at risk for a diagnosis of an ASD, we now have early intervention services that can be extremely helpful for infants, toddlers, and preschoolers with autism spectrum disorders. The sooner you get a diagnosis for your son or daughter, the sooner you can arrange for services from trained professionals who are attuned to child development and know how to adapt ABA technology to very young children. These professionals can not only work directly with your child, but also teach you the necessary skills to work with him or her at home.

Resources

You will want to locate the **early intervention services in your own state.** This link, which is part of the NECTAC website, is updated yearly to identify the coordinator of IDEA Part C services in each state: www.nectac.org/contact/ptccoord.asp

The National Dissemination Center for Children with Disabilities has many articles on early intervention, IFSPs, natural environments, etc. in both English and Spanish. You can find them under the "Babies and Toddlers" tab on their website: www.nichcy.org

NECTAC *is the National Early Childhood Technical Assistance Center, which is supported by the U.S. Department of Education's Office of Special Education Programs (OSEP) under the provisions of the Individuals with Disabilities Education Act (IDEA). Their website address is:* www.nectac.org

The **U.S. Department of Education Office of Special Education** has a useful website on IDEA. The address is: http://www2.ed.gov/about/offices/list/osers/osep/index.html?src=mr. They also host a website at http://idea.ed.gov, which may be easier to access.

Mayerson and Associates have a website with useful information and many links to other organizations involved in services to people with ASD. Their website address is: www.mayerslaw.com

Hinkle, Fingles, & Prior offer useful information about advocacy for people with ASD and planning for the future of children on the spectrum. Their website address is: www.hinkle1.com

Peter and Pamela Wright are adjunct professors of law at the William and Mary Law School. Their website is a good resource for the latest on the rights of children with ASD and their families. It also provides good background on ASD: www.wrightslaw.com

5 | Helping Your Child Relate: Essential Skills

The Randolph Family

It wasn't until their second child was born that Gayle and Anthony Randolph began to notice the subtle social behavior that had been missing with their first son, Ethan. By the time he was a few months old, their second child, Marcus, watched their faces and returned their smiles and expressions. As a toddler, Marcus turned to greet his parents whenever they walked into a room, and came running with a big smile when they returned from work at the end of the day. These very early social skills were a big part of who Marcus was. He had the natural ability to connect with and convey interest and excitement to his parents without using words.

Looking back, Gayle and Anthony realized that Ethan had not ever made these social connections—not when he was very young or even now as he was growing older. As the differences sank in, they were overwhelmed with a sense of loss for their first son.

When Ethan was very young, the Randolphs had focused on so many things—including keeping him healthy and safe and watching his skills develop—that the missing social behavior was not obvious to them. Like most new parents, Gayle and Anthony had marveled at their son's early development, as well as his idiosyncrasies. Later, when they started to be concerned about Ethan's development, they had focused on more obvious behaviors, such as hand flapping and tantrums. They had also noticed his unique and fascinating skills, such as his intense interest in objects, letters, numbers, and complex puzzles. These were the signs and symptoms that led them to seek an assessment from the developmental pediatrician.

For these reasons, Gayle and Anthony had overlooked the early social signs of Ethan's ASD, but the differences were obvious when they *looked back in time. It tugged at Gayle's heart when Marcus brought her his favorite stuffed animal when she was resting, and when he showed her his finger if he had a boo-boo. Ethan did not show or share anything with her unless he needed help. For instance, he would bring a container of toys for her to open for him. Even when he used actions to request help, Ethan did not use eye contact, facial expression, and words or sounds to clarify what he wanted the way Marcus did.*

Now that Gayle could see the behaviors that her older son was missing, she wondered if she could go back and help him learn those skills. Fortunately, the provider of Ethan's early intervention services had experience using empirically supported methods to work on social skills. She actually began Ethan's treatment by teaching Gayle and Anthony to encourage and foster the social connection behaviors that would be the building blocks of Ethan's future social development.

Introduction

Recognizing and understanding the building blocks for social interaction is the first step in addressing the challenges to children with ASD. Through intensive and early intervention, young children with ASD can make significant progress in these basic foundation skills.

With typical development, all interactions contribute to a child's social skills, beginning in infancy. Children learn to associate social

contact with very basic needs as their caregivers provide them with food, warmth, and comfort. Babies learn from their environment by watching other people's faces for their expressions, and by following their parents' eye gaze to contact the world around them. Even before they have words, children begin to learn the value of other people as sources of information and also to share information by using

Social Development Milestones

Birth to 3 months	Infants show interest in their caregivers, smile, and respond to touch and social interaction
3 to 6 months	Babies begin to smile and laugh in response to simple social interaction like peek-a-boo or hearing their name, and also initiate simple interactions with eye gaze, smiles, and laughter.
6 to 9 months	Babies make clear responses to language and gestures and show a wider range of emotions, expressing enjoyment as well as displeasure. Babies respond differently to strangers and familiar people.
9 to 12 months	Babies may show anxiety when separated from their caregivers and develop attachments to comfort objects. They also begin to imitate simple actions.
1 to 2 years	Toddlers interact with others to express affection and show helpfulness and assertiveness. They may show pride in accomplishments and recognize and respond to their own face in photos or a mirror.
2 to 3 years	Children develop a stronger sense of self, show curiosity, evaluate themselves, and may label themselves (good, bad, big, boy/girl). They develop play interests and participate in some group activities. They may show a variety of moods, talk about feelings, and develop fears.
3 to 4 years	Children show more interest in other children and initiate play, sharing, and turn taking with help. They are more independent in self-care and in following directions with reminders.
4 to 5 years	Children begin to develop friendships and moral reasoning, such as understanding fairness and recognizing others' feelings and perspectives.

their eyes and faces. The table on page 65 gives an overview of when and how these social milestones typically develop in young children.

Which Social Skills Are Hardest for Young Children with ASD?

Decades of research and work have helped us develop a good understanding of some of the critical social deficits for young children with autism spectrum disorders. One treatment model, called the *Early Start Denver Model (ESDM)*, was developed to focus specifically on the key areas of social skills that are difficult for children with ASD at a very young age. Sally Rogers and Geraldine Dawson, the developers of the model, list these areas in their book (Rogers, Dawson, & Vismara, 2012):

- Paying attention to other people (including through eye contact)
- Using social smiles
- Taking turns and engaging in social play
- Using gestures and language
- Imitating others
- Coordinating attention (eye gaze) with others
- Playing in typical ways with toys

All children with ASD have some difficulty in these areas, as they are central to the diagnosis. For many young children, however, these

problems may be very subtle, or they may have other strengths that make these deficits less noticeable. For example, a child who can speak and has a strong interest in certain activities may seem very successful when playing in familiar or preferred ways. But difficulties may be noticeable when he is interacting with other children in situations where each person needs to respond flexibly to the others' words and actions.

Most of the skills in the list above are social behaviors that typically develop in the first years of life. Addressing these fundamental skills when a child is very young and has first been diagnosed or identified as being at risk for ASD is very important. These skills are crucial because social interaction is part of most other activities in life as children grow. They are essential for play and for developing friendships, as well as for learning from others and learning how the social world works. Without an understanding of underlying social concepts such as sharing attention and reciprocity, children have great difficulty interacting successfully—whether to get their basic needs met or to establish meaningful friendships.

Early Intervention and Treatment

Thanks to an increased awareness of the more subtle social signs of autism spectrum disorders, professionals are turning to intervention at a much earlier age—as soon as an ASD is diagnosed or suspected. When you are new to the world of autism, it may seem unnatural to begin any intervention when a child is still so young. You may have this perception because for many years, ASD was not diagnosed until children were much older, and the treatments that people wrote about were used with older children.

However, just as the field has been able to make great strides in identifying ASD at a much younger age, there is also research to show that strategies and treatments can be adapted and applied to even younger children. Research has also shown that intense focus on building age appropriate social, play, and communication interactions very early on can help make a huge impact on the later development of children with ASD. While *early intensive behavioral intervention (EIBI)* used to refer to treatment in the preschool years following a child's diagnosis, there is more research now on the impact of teaching strategies with children in the early intervention years, before preschool.

Key social, communication, and play skills are closely related to each other from early in development. As discussed in Chapter 3, one treatment model—*Pivotal Response Training*—was developed with a specific focus on these underlying "pivotal" skill areas. Developed by Lynn and Robert Koegel, PRT is a well-researched treatment strategy that is based on the principles of applied behavior analysis. It is designed to build skills that are central to a broad range of behaviors that a child needs. For example, to begin helping young children with ASD improve social skills, parents or therapists learn to attract or capture the child's attention to an object or activity that is motivating.

Let's say that Sam really enjoys bubbles, and may run over to them or reach out to them when his mother blows them. Sam's treatment team decides to use this interest in bubbles to initiate interactions with Sam, get his attention, and establish an activity that can be the basis of many important learning exchanges. Sam's mother might repeatedly blow bubbles between her face and her son's face and make an exaggerated "pop!" noise as she makes a wide-eyed and open-mouthed expression. After many repetitions of this action, Sam might begin to look to his mother's face to see if she will make the expression when the bubble pops again, and this can be the basis of joint attention.

One important difference between a child with ASD and one who is not at risk for ASD is that a child who is developing typically is often immediately aware of his mother's reaction and seeks to repeat it. A child with ASD might require many repetitions of the action in the same context before he becomes aware of and anticipates his mother's reaction as part of the sequence. This is why part of the intervention process involves making these action-reaction sequences more noticeable and predictable by exaggerating and repeating them over and over. The next step is to help the child learn to produce a specific action (word, sound, gesture) to participate with, or obtain, the motivating item. Many research studies have demonstrated that this strategy is successful for children with ASD.

Of course, PRT is not the only treatment model to use naturally occurring motivation and the concept of reinforcement. However, the PRT model is extensively researched and has been described in many manuals and research articles.

Teaching about the Reciprocal Nature of Social Interactions

The specific focus of treatment when working on early social skills with children with autism is on building interest in and awareness of the reciprocal nature of social interaction. In a reciprocal social interaction, the people who are interacting are having an effect on each other. For example, in a game of peek-a-boo, Daddy hides and then shows his face, saying "boo!" His daughter laughs and either reaches to cover his face again, wanting him to repeat the game, or covers her face to be the "hider." Both father and daughter enjoy the reactions that their own actions bring about in the other person.

In other words, instruction for children with ASD is aimed at teaching young children that other people's reactions—their facial expressions, eyes, movements, and language—are meaningful and enjoyable.

Typically developing children learn about the pleasures of social interactions naturally. They don't need to learn *how* to participate in a game of peek-a-boo; they naturally seek to repeat the game and continue with the back-and-forth of the interaction. However, when children don't naturally pick up this understanding, research has shown that we can build these skills though the children's interactions with loved ones.

Intervention to build these foundation skills begins with providing intensive, specific, and structured experiences. For example, you might introduce a very simple play or social routine, such as saying "I'm gonna getcha!" and reaching out to tickle your child. You can repeat this interaction many times, highlighting or exaggerating the motions, expressions, and steps leading up to the tickle. As your child learns to anticipate the tickle, you can insert a pause, and wait for some indication that your child is anticipating the next action. After some action from your child, the game will continue. At first, the action might just be to lift his shirt for a belly tickle, or a sound, or reaching toward your hand.

Over time, you can wait for this response from your child or use gentle prompting (covered in Chapter 3) to help him learn a new response that will continue the game. Continuing with the peek-a-boo example, early instruction might involve gently prompting your child to cover his eyes to initiate a turn with peek-a-boo.

These examples illustrate that the activities themselves are not unlike the social games parents typically play with their young kids. The very important difference, however, is that with ASD intervention, these activities are done with specific goals in mind, and need to be structured and repeated intentionally to create many learning opportunities.

Many of the successful treatment methods for helping children with ASD develop these early social skills are built from the same concepts. These treatment approaches come from watching how children interact with the world and understanding how behavior is learned. Many of the most successful and well-researched treatment strategies, including PRT, are rooted in applied behavior analysis.

Another treatment approach successfully used to teach social skills to the littlest learners is the *Early Start Denver Model,* introduced in Chapter 2. The ESDM describes a number of steps that you can take to capture your child's attention, provide an activity or stimulation that

---

Example: "Learning to Fly!"

Imagine that you have discovered that your child enjoys being swung around in the air like an airplane. He giggles and smiles when you randomly pick him up and swing him, but he makes no attempts to ask you to keep the game going when you stop. You can use his fondness for this activity to gradually and systematically teach him to ask to continue and eventually request these and other activities.

You might start teaching this skill by using a simple phrase before you lift your child and begin the game. For example, you say, "Time for take-off!" and then swing him around in the air. At first, you might turn a few times and then "come in for a landing." Then you pause, watch your child's face, and repeat again, "Time for take-off!" and spin him. Gradually, you insert pauses after the landing until your child glances at you and immediately "take-off" again as soon as he makes brief eye contact. Once your child makes eye contact regularly to get another "flight," you can "up the ante" by waiting a little bit longer for him to make a sound or say a word. Sometimes this pause is the hardest part, but an experienced therapist can help you learn how to establish a strong enough routine and wait long enough for your child to make some type of response to show that he wants more of the activity.

pleases him, and motivate him to continue to interact with you and make requests. In this treatment model, clinicians and parents focus on developing social routines that interest the child and gradually build a format for turn-taking and shared experience. The box on page 70 describes a simple example from the ESDM model that involves identifying a social or physical routine that your child enjoys.

Joint Attention. Other basic social skills, such as joint attention skills, can also be systematically taught to young children with ASD. These include the skills of:

1. responding to "bids" for joint attention (the child looks at what others are trying to show him), and
2. initiating joint attention (the child attracts someone's attention to something that he finds interesting).

Many researchers have shown that these components of joint attention can be taught by breaking the skill down and teaching it systematically. For example, Christina Whalen and Laura Schreibman did a series of studies in which they gradually taught joint attention to very young children with ASD. Breaking the behavior of joint attention down into its components allowed the instructors to work on the skill piece by piece. First they helped children learn to respond to someone who was touching or showing them an object. Next, they taught them to attend to a person's eye gaze to notice something. After the children learned these responsive skills, they were successfully taught how to initiate attracting another person's attention.

Sharing Activities. Another concept that is fundamental to basic social skills is the notion that events can become more interesting or more fun when they are shared. Imagine that you just got wonderful news or just accomplished something you have been working hard on. For most of us, and for typically developing young children, it is second nature to find someone to tell—to share your excitement, pride, or happiness. For children with ASD, this does not happen naturally. Of course, many parents of young children with ASD know what their child enjoys. But this is because they have observed their child, not because the child engages his parents in his excitement.

Children with ASD are much less likely to call another person's attention to something they are looking at or enjoying. Some children with ASD may have certain interests or topics that are extremely exciting to them and that they wish to share with others, but often these interests do not develop until later and may be limited to very specific and sometimes unusual topics. With careful attention and intensive intervention, children with ASD can learn to share activities with others, rather than engage in solitary or isolated play.

In a recent research study, Ty Vernon and his colleagues (2012) used an intervention that produced important changes in parent-child eye contact and shared enjoyment of an activity. In this study, parents of children with ASD were trained in PRT and learned to give their children access to an item or activity in exchange for a certain response. In addition, the parents learned to join the activity, even if it was not a social activity to begin with. For example, if a child was shown part of a favorite video playing a song, the parent sang along with the song as well. By inserting themselves into these motivating activities, parents were able to get their children to make more eye contact and to direct more positive facial expressions their way.

Later Social Skills

As children with ASD grow older, instruction often switches to helping them develop more of the mechanics of social interactions. For example, many young children with ASD are taught how to respond to greetings or questions, how to look at someone when their name is called, how to attend to a teacher or parent for instruction, and how to take turns or engage in other behaviors that show respect for others. Applied behavior analysis has a long history of developing these behaviors in children of all ages and at different skill levels.

As children with ASD learn other skills, they are helped to apply skills in new situations and settings with others, including other children. However, the underlying concepts of social interest, value, and reciprocity must continually be addressed. Research has shown that these core aspects of social skills *can* be built over time, beginning as early as possible.

Encouraging Social Interest at Home

For parents of young children with ASD, it can be very disheartening to try to interact with their child only to have him ignore their attempts or react negatively. You will, of course, want to seek out a professional who can help you and your child enjoy a more typical

parent/child relationship. Finding someone who can help guide you in building your child's social interest and awareness is an essential step. However, the most significant part of addressing your child's social skills will be keeping these concepts in mind during your daily interaction with him.

Identifying natural opportunities to insert yourself into your child's activities is a skill you can develop as a parent. This will require different skills than those you may use naturally with your other children. For example, if your child resists your attempts to join his play, you will need to step back and think about why your child may be reacting this way. Often, parents are eager to teach new skills, make requests, or ask questions when they join their children's play. This is not a problem for a typically developing child. But a child with ASD may perceive this type of parent involvement as adding demands or difficulties to the activity. Instead, you need to find ways to join your child's activity that enhance it in his view.

The key is to add a new, fun element to the activity that involves you. By slowly inserting and repeating these elements, you can establish yourself as a fun and important part of their play. For example, let's say that your child enjoys bubbles, music, a particular video, or playing in sand or water (the bathtub is a great place for social play!). Below are a few simple examples to illustrate the general concept of enhancing these activities:

- Add silly or new sound effects and facial expressions.
- Add new physical components (tickles, being lifted in the air, etc.).
- Add new or unexpected items (use a small animal figure to try to pop or catch bubbles or try a battery-powered bubble wand; use a toy traffic cone as a microphone).

If your child has a very intense and specific interest in a certain activity, it would probably be best not to start by trying to insert yourself into that activity because he may become upset if you try to change it.

Keep in mind that this process of helping your child enjoy interaction with you will not happen in one play session; it will take time. Unlike with specific skills such as tying a shoe or putting a puzzle together, social skills are always different and always changing, and continually evolve over time.

References

Rogers, S. J., Dawson, G., & Vismara, L. (2012). *An early start for your child with autism*. New York, NY: Guilford Press.

Vernon, T. W, Koegel, R. L., Dauterman, H., & Stolen, K. (2012). An early social engagement intervention for young children with autism and their parents. *Journal of Autism and Developmental Disorders, 42*, 2702-2717.

Whalen, C., & Schreibman, L. (2003). Joint attention training for children with autism using behavior modification procedures. *Journal of Child Psychology and Psychiatry, 44*(3), 456-68.

6 | Give Your Child a Voice: Speech, Sign, and Other Methods

The Castellanos Family

Demitri and Alicia Castellanos came from a large, close family. They lived with their three children—ten-year-old Carmen, seven-year-old Marco, and two-year-old Max—as well as Demitri's mother, Maria. Mealtimes were loud and busy, with Carmen and Marco excitedly sharing tales of their lives and getting into typical sibling arguments. Often, more than one conversation was going on at once. Max contributed very few sounds to the din, but at first, the family just assumed there was so much going on that he didn't have a chance to get a word in edgewise.

Max seemed content and often entertained himself with his favorite belongings or with the television. In many ways, it was easy for Maria to care for him during the day while the older kids were at school and Dimitri and Alicia were at work. But over the last six months, the adults had become increasingly concerned because they did not see Max developing language the way Carmen and Marco had.

Carmen had been speaking from the moment she could make sounds. Even when she didn't know any words as a young toddler, she used sounds and expressions to have "conversations" with her family. She often gestured with her hands and used facial expressions just as the adults around the table did. Marco had taken much longer to talk, but was a busy and active boy. Compared to his sister, he had been more likely to engage his family by climbing, jumping, tickling, or physical antics before he developed language effectively. He was still less of a talker than his sister.

But Max's quietness was different than Marco's. He did not participate in conversations with sounds or with his eyes, face, or body. Sometimes he seemed to watch others when they spoke, but other times *he didn't seem to notice. His family knew that he could make sounds and had even heard some words, but these were fleeting. Sometimes they heard what they thought was a word but then never heard it again.*

It was for these speech concerns that the Castellanos sought evaluation and treatment for Max. He was diagnosed with ASD and soon after began receiving speech and developmental interventions through an early intervention program. When the therapist came to meet with Demitri, Alicia, and Maria, she explained how closely connected communication and social skills were, and that her work with Max would focus on these two areas together. She would work with the three of them to develop strategies they could use to help Max be more motivated and successful in communicating with others.

Introduction

Communication difficulties are one of the primary symptoms of an autism spectrum disorder. However, there are huge differences in just how communication is affected in each individual with ASD. There are children who do not make any sounds or words at all, as well as children who have the ability to speak but do not use their speech to communicate with others in typical ways.

Depending on each individual child's unique profile, treatment starts in a different place but uses the same underlying strategies. In general, early treatment focuses on helping children understand that all the language we use has an impact on the environment around us. Treatment for very young children with ASD starts by helping them learn this connection—that their actions (words, sounds, or gestures) can change their environment. For example, reaching up to Mom can lead to being picked up or making the sound "buh" can lead to more bubbles.

Much has been written about teaching language to children with ASD. People have been studying this for decades, long before there was research on how to build and develop social skills. Reviewing the information that is available about teaching language to children with ASD can be overwhelming. Not only has there been a lot of research, but there are many different teaching strategies and not all professionals use the same terms for what and how they teach.

The most important point to keep in mind is that ***early language instruction needs to help a child have some control over, and a way*** *to connect with, the world around her.* Strategies that emphasize teaching in the natural environment—which are the focus of this book—all involve making language instruction meaningful. This is a concept that has been emphasized by autism researchers for almost 40 years (Harris, 1975)!

This chapter discusses the basic process of building communication skills in young children with ASD. We will highlight the overall process and goals of communication intervention, compare and contrast some models of intervention you may encounter, and discuss what the field has learned from decades of research in this area.

Communication Milestones in Typical Development

Long before children learn to speak, they interact and communicate with the world around them. As discussed in the chapter on social skills, communication and social interaction go hand in hand, particularly in the early stages of development. When parents reflect on their child's development of communication skills, many focus on their

Typical Language Development	
Birth to 3 months	Reacts to sound and speech, makes "cooing" or pleasure sounds, has different "cries" for different needs
4 to 6 months	Follows sources of sounds with eyes and responds to music, changes in tone of voice, and toys that make sounds. Also laughs and babbles using speech sounds
7 months to 1 year	Responds to/understands simple words and requests; makes simple gestures (arms up to be held), imitates speech sounds, has one or two words
1 to 2 years	Knows some body parts and simple requests and questions, learns new words regularly, points to pictures or objects when named, puts two words together
2 to 3 years	Uses 2- to 3-word utterances and requests objects by naming them or pointing them out; speech is understood by family
3 to 4 years	Answers simple "wh" questions, uses sentences of 4 + words, talks about activities

child's first word(s) or on when they first begin to put words together. In this chapter, we will focus not only on the words, sounds, or actions children make to communicate, but also on the context. That is, what are the situations in which your child is communicating and why?

As you can see from the table summarizing typical development, babies learn within their first year of life that they can have an impact on their surroundings by behaving in certain ways. For example, they learn that crying leads to food, warmth, or comfort by a caregiver, and reaching up toward a parent can lead to being held. These are important ways of communicating that do not involve words or speech.

Communication Skills in Children with ASD

Children with ASD are often missing these fundamental communication behaviors or use them only rarely. Most often, young children with ASD do not convey their needs to other people using gestures,

eye contact, or sounds. For example, a child with ASD may bring a broken toy to her parent, but not make eye contact, sounds, or words to "ask" for help. In contrast, a child *without* ASD would be much more likely to show the toy to her parent, make eye contact between the item and her parent (joint attention), give a questioning look, and possibly make sounds or try to approximate words ("happen?" as in, "what happened?").

Children with ASD are often delayed in both the process of producing speech (sounds, words, phrases) and in the communication behaviors and actions that accompany speech or occur even before speech develops. These behaviors include gestures, eye contact, facial expressions, and back-and-forth "exchanges" of gestures, glances, or words with another person.

Because the ability to communicate with others is central to all future learning, learning to communicate basic needs is the starting place of intervention in ASD. Establishing a system of communication is essential to building later social skills. Imagine not being able to let someone know that you are feeling sick or sad or hungry, or that you want or don't want something. Often, it is the inability to communicate effectively that sets the stage for a child's behavior problems. Usually challenging behavior has its roots in a child's inability to express something or to control her environment. Building fundamental communication skills very early will help prevent challenging behavior to begin with or support efforts to address existing behavior difficulties.

Because of the central role that communication plays in behavior, it is not uncommon for parents to teach their very young children *without* ASD some simple sign language or gestures. This can help children communicate even before they begin to use speech. Building communication strategies very early in development can help avoid behavior problems and teach a child the value of communicating using appropriate behavior.

Language as "Verbal Behavior"

One theory of language that provides a solid foundation for building communication skills in children with autism spectrum disorders is the theory of Verbal Behavior. This well-researched theory was first described by the famous psychologist and researcher B. F. Skinner in 1957. Skinner's theory emphasized that communication is essentially behavior that is developed and maintained because of how the communication behavior affects the world around us. For example, a young child might hear her father say "ball" when the two of them are playing with a ball together. She then imitates him, and also says "ball" when she sees a ball. This behavior is strengthened because her father tells her, "Yes! That's a ball!" and praises her when she says the word. Skinner's theory emphasized how similar language is to other behavior. For example, throwing, rolling, or catching the ball are also things the girl will see her father do, and she will receive praise for imitating those behaviors as well.

This Verbal Behavior theory of language is very important in ABA treatment. Using this theory to develop language intervention helps us focus on arranging situations in such a way that a child will be more likely to use certain communicative behaviors. These behaviors can then be rewarded and reinforced. For example, it is more likely that your child will learn to say "Up!" and reach up if she gets picked up every time she says "up" and reaches up toward an adult. You can help your child develop this behavior by creating many planned opportunities to practice the skill.

As children with ASD develop communication skills, the Verbal Behavior concept can be applied to encourage them to use more advanced language. For example, adults can create opportunities for a child to request a snack and then specify how many, what size, or what color. That is, after the child has the skill to ask for a snack ("fruit snacks!"), her parents can build practice asking, "which color?" so that the child can choose between red or green, for example. This reinforces the idea that by using more language, a child can get access to more of what she wants.

What Type of Communication?

The first step in building your child's communication skills is to figure out the best mode of communication for her at the present time. This is critical for helping your child learn how to communicate and to have some control over her environment. Remember, whatever strategy or mode of communication is chosen at first, it does not mean this will be the way your child communicates forever. However, it is important to start by teaching your child to use behavior or responses that she can already make. This increases the chances that she will be successful in communicating and be rewarded for her attempts.

Once your child solidly understands how communication *works*, she can learn more words or more complex ways to communicate. But in the beginning, the focus is on teaching the concept that she can make some sort of response (a word, sound, or gesture) that can affect what happens around her.

Communicating with Sign Language or Pictures

Some children with ASD can only make a few sounds when they begin intervention and they don't seem to be able to make them on command or in response to a model or request. That is, you might hear the child say a sound like "buh," but when you say "buh" to the child, she doesn't imitate it. For these children, progress in making sounds or words may be very slow or difficult and can lead to frustration for both the parent and the child. In this situation, the child is often taught to use a method or mode of communication other than speech so she can have an impact on her environment (or, in other words, ask for things she wants or needs).

Two methods of non-vocal communication are commonly used with young children with ASD: pictures and manual signs. For these children, learning to use an unspoken communication system is critical because it helps them use language-based exchanges to communicate with others. It will be important for them to communicate by using a behavior they can already perform.

PECS. Psychologist Andy Bondy and speech-language pathologist Lori Frost (2002) have developed a successful method of communicating without speech based on the Verbal Behavior theory of language. This method is called the Picture Exchange Communication System (PECS). When used according to their carefully planned and well-researched protocol, PECS can be extremely successful in teaching children to communicate by exchanging pictures with a listener. There are research

studies showing that many children are able to develop verbal communication at the same time they learn to communicate using PECS.

To use PECS, communication partners physically "exchange" (hand to each other) small photographs or line drawings in order to communicate. In early stages of training, the child is taught to exchange pictures that will help her get her needs met. For example, she learns to hand over pictures of desired snacks or toys to indicate what she wants to eat or play with. As the child becomes more skilled at communicating, she learns to construct sentences using several pictures to express her desires, make comments, and answer questions. Central to the PECS system is that it focuses on the child learning to initiate communication with others.

For more information about using PECS, you may want to consult another book in the Woodbine House autism series, *A Picture's Worth* (Bondy & Frost, 2002).

Sign Language. Another Verbal Behavior approach to teaching communication to children who are not ready to use speech relies on sign language. Typically, young children with ASD at this stage of instruction are taught standard signs for common objects and actions that they might ask for (similar to the early pictures used for PECS). A child who is not able to make the standard sign for something may learn to use an approximation or simpler version of the sign.

Psychologists Mark Sundberg and James Partington (1998) have published a guide to early language and communication instruction for children with ASD and focus on using sign language when spoken language is difficult for a young child. As is the case with PECS, there are research studies showing that sign training can support the development of spoken language of youngsters with ASD.

Choosing the Right Approach. Currently, there is no consensus or solid research confirming that either approach (sign or PECS) is better than the other. When thinking about what is best for your child, here are several factors to consider:

- *Your child's skills.* For example, if she has good fine motor skills, sign language might be appropriate. If she is a strong visual learner, PECS might work well for her.
- *Your child's preferences.* There is some preliminary research showing that some children who are taught both signs

and picture exchange for a few simple items may show a preference for one approach when they are given a choice of how to communicate.

- *The experience of the early intervention provider.* Often, a professional will have more experience using one approach than another and may suggest using the approach with which she is most familiar.

- *The willingness and ability of your child's family, friends, and community members to learn* to understand and respond to signs or pictures. While most people can understand PECS without formal training, sign language requires communication partners to know at least as many signs as the child does.

- *The portability of the system.* Someone who uses signs always has her system—her hands with her—whereas PECS symbols may not be useable in some environments such as a swimming pool.

Importantly, children with ASD can usually learn to communicate successfully with others using either approach, as long as the person overseeing the teaching makes sure to:

- *Understand the environment and communication context.* This involves having a therapist who carefully creates situations to set the stage for communication, such as putting preferred snacks or items in clear containers or just slightly out of reach so that the child has many opportunities to ask for them.

- *Carefully keep data to track progress.* For example, a therapist should track how well the child communicates, and also keep track of how much help she needs. Monitoring these data over time will ensure that there is an objective measure of progress or lack thereof.

Encouraging Speech. In many cases, children with ASD who use signs or PECS will begin to develop spoken language as well.

If your child is being taught to use a non-vocal approach such as PECS or signing for communication, the early intervention therapists will still often work on trying to increase your child's sound productions overall. For example, they may use procedures in which they repeatedly say a sound or word while your child is taking part in very motivating activities. A number of clinicians and researchers have shown that this can increase how often a child says certain sounds or words. Sometimes these strategies can help the child to say more sounds and give her more experience making the sounds, so that they can then be worked on more formally in a teaching program.

Using Technology to Assist with Communication. A speech therapist with experience using augmentative communication systems (ACS) will have information about how and when to introduce technology to assist in communication. The development of affordable and portable devices such as tablets or iPads has made technology a more available option for many youngsters with communication difficulties.

To date, there is not much research on how the use of technology affects communication learning at the earliest stages. But there are many examples of how these devices can be used successfully *after* a child has mastered the process of communication with another system such as PECS or sign. It is important to keep in mind that in early communication instruction we want children to learn to communicate with people in their surroundings, not to interact with a device. Introducing technology at an early stage may interfere with the social communication focus. Often, however, devices such as iPads can be very powerful motivators or reinforcers and can be used during instruction that way.

Communicating with Speech

Some young children with autism spectrum disorders already make vocal sounds, say words, or even put more than one word together. If your child already makes sounds or tries to say words and can imitate them when asked to, then intervention will begin by focusing on using vocal communication (ordinary speech).

If your child already shows the ability to produce words and can begin to put words together, formal instruction is very important. Your child will need to work on building vocabulary and increasing the use of these words in context. In other words, she will need to learn not only what words mean, but even more importantly, when and how to use these words with others in social situations. Your child may benefit from the services of a speech-language pathologist for individual instruction in communication skills, but also therapy in small group situations so she can learn to communicate with other children when she is ready for that more advanced skill.

When and How to Teach Communication

Early in the history of ABA treatment, well-known researchers and clinicians worked on helping children develop communication skills in both highly structured settings and in more natural settings. Sometimes formal settings for language instruction were used because children started treatment much later than is common now. This means that many children with ASD received intervention in school settings rather than in their homes.

Research has shown that many children with ASD need an ongoing balance of naturalistic and more structured ABA teaching methods. The research-based teaching methods that are most likely to help young children with autism succeed in learning communication skills are:

- *Discrete Trial Instruction (DTI).* DTI is used to target new skills in a focused and structured way. This is one of the primary methods that was used when ABA methods were first employed with children with ASD. It involves teaching specific language goals and other skills in a very structured environment with minimal distractions. As originally used, DTI also involved many repetitions in teaching.

And these naturalistic methods which share many of the same features:

- *Incidental Teaching.* Incidental Teaching (Hart & Risley, 1968; McGee, 1999) is an approach that emphasizes recognizing or creating learning situations that occur naturally, and providing opportunities for children to use more elaborate language. For example, a child who is playing with blocks can first learn to ask for a block, and then be encouraged to elaborate her requests by asking for "the blue block" or "the big block." Incidental Teaching was not specifically developed for use with children with ASD.

- *Natural Language Paradigm (NLP).* Natural Language Paradigm (Koegel, O'Dell, & Koegel, 1987) extends the concept of Incidental Teaching and adapts and applies the strategies specifically to children with autism. This approach also shares some of the specific strategies that are used in DTI, including simplifying the cues or instructions given to the child and providing prompts and reinforcement (as discussed in Chapter 3). However, NLP uses these strategies in a less structured, more natural setting (compared to DTI).

- *Natural Environment Training (NET).* Natural Environment Training (Sundberg and Partington, 1998) is a strategy that focuses on the use of Skinner's Verbal Behavior theory of language (described earlier in this chapter). It emphasizes beginning instruction with teaching "mands" (i.e., a word or behavior that allows the child to get what she wants or needs) in everyday situations, and arranging or contriving frequent opportunities to use mands throughout the child's activities.

- *Pivotal Response Training (PRT).* Pivotal Response Training (Koegel & Koegel, 2006) is discussed in Chapters 3 and 5. PRT developed as an extension of NLP, and focuses on embedding learning opportunities within motivating activities. In addition to focusing on language, PRT, like NLP, also addresses other skills that are essential for children with autism to learn, such as attending to many cues in the environment, initiating interactions, etc.

In all of these naturalistic strategies, one of the first situations in which a therapist will try to teach your child to use words, manual signs, or picture exchange is when she is making requests. According to Skinner's theory of Verbal Behavior, the technical term for requesting is "manding." In this situation, when a child is indicating that she wants something by reaching or making a sound, the therapist or parent will encourage

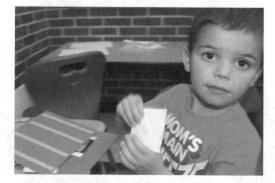

a simple word or approximation to request the item (e.g., "cracker" or "kuh-kuh"). With both sign and picture exchange, the child is taught to make a manual sign or exchange a specific picture to receive the item.

Rather than teaching your child many vocabulary words and having her label many things in isolation, the focus will be on teaching words in the actual situations where she is naturally motivated to communicate.

Encouraging Requests at Home

Here are some tips you can keep in mind to create lots of opportunities for your child to make requests (mand) for things.

Do:

- Find ways to encourage requesting, even in well-known routines. For example, if your child always wants juice instead of milk, you could still bring out both containers and ask her to indicate which she wants, rather than just automatically giving her the juice. You could also have more than one juice available for her to request.
- When possible, remind yourself to pause and wait for your child to make some indication of what she wants before you provide it.
- Put items out of reach but within sight, or store items in clear containers that your child needs help opening.
- Practice requesting in all situations you can, not just during teaching sessions.

Don't:

- Push too hard. Keep the request (mand) simple and make sure it is something your child can do. For example, don't expect a two-word phrase if your child is not yet consistently using one word to make requests.
- Prompt too soon. This can be tough to figure out sometimes. You don't want to wait until your child gets frustrated, but you also need to pause and let your child recognize that she can do something or *should* do something to get the item or activity.

Summary

It is important to focus on finding and creating as many learning opportunities as possible for teaching your child to communicate. Remember, every interaction a young child has with her environment is an opportunity for learning, and the goal of early intervention is to carefully focus and orchestrate these numerous learning opportunities in natural settings throughout the day. This does not mean that there isn't value to building vocabulary in other contexts besides making requests. Of course, children with ASD eventually need to learn words for things they are not requesting, but this type of language instruction is a secondary priority at the early stages of teaching. What very young children need most of all is to learn how to interact with others about the things that are most important to them in everyday life.

References

Bondy, A., & Frost, L. (2002). *A picture's worth: PECS and other visual communication strategies in autism*. Bethesda, MD: Woodbine House.

Harris, S. L. (1975). Teaching *language* to nonverbal children: With emphasis on problems of generalization. *Psychological Bulletin, 82*, 564-580.

Hart, B. M., & Risley, T.R. (1968). Establishing use of descriptive adjectives in the spontaneous speech of disadvantaged preschool children. *Journal of Applied Behavior Analysis, 1*, 109-120.

Koegel, R. L., & Koegel, L. K. (2006). *Pivotal response treatments for autism*. Baltimore, MD: Paul Brookes.

Koegel, R. L., O'Dell, M. C., & Koegel, L. K. (1987). A natural language teaching paradigm for nonverbal autistic children. *Journal of Autism and Developmental Disorders, 17*, 187-200.

Koegel, R. L., & Koegel, L. K. (2006). *Pivotal response treatments for autism: Communication, social, and academic development*. Baltimore, MD: Paul Brookes.

McGee, G. G., Morrier, M. J., & Daly, T. (1999). An incidental teaching approach to early intervention for toddlers with autism. *Research and Practice for Persons with Severe Disabilities, 24*(3), 133-146.

Skinner, B. F. (1957). *Verbal Behavior*. Englewood Cliffs, NJ: Prentice Hall.

Sundberg, M. L., & Partington, J. W. (1996). *Teaching language to children with autism or other developmental disabilities*. Pleasant Hill, CA: Behavior Analysts, Inc.

7 | Why Work on Play?
Benefits for You and Your Child

The Nagy Family

Merrill and Raphael Nagy had been delighted when they learned they were expecting twins. Much as they had anticipated, the first year after the birth of Chloe and Michael was both rewarding and exhausting. The Nagys enjoyed watching their children change and grow, and they filled their home with brightly colored toys and decorations. During the twins' early years, Chloe and Michael both spent time exploring their surroundings and toys, putting items in their mouths, banging them together or on the floor, and eventually taking things apart and putting them back together.

As the children grew, however, Merrill and Raphael noticed that Michael ignored many of his newer toys and that he did not seem interested in new gifts. Sometimes he did not even open a brightly colored package. Instead, Michael preferred a small number of familiar toys. He mostly played with his favorite vehicles, arranging them in certain ways. He got angry and cried when his sister or his parents tried to engage with him or the toys. Chloe, on the other hand, sought out her parents during play, often imitating their actions and directing sounds and words to them.

Although the Nagys had heard from many friends and relatives that boys develop differently than girls do, they were convinced that there was more to be concerned about. When they shared their concerns and observations about their son's difficulties with language, play, and social interactions with their pediatrician, he recommended they take Michael to a developmental pediatrician or local autism treatment center for an evaluation. Merrill and Raphael were devastated but not surprised when the follow-up evaluation resulted in a diagnosis of ASD for Michael. Thanks to their early recognition of the differences in development between Michael and his twin sister, their son was able to begin early intervention at the age of 18 months.

Since Michael was so young, the Nagys were initially concerned about how he could participate in therapy or treatment. Many of the treatments they had heard about and read about online seemed to be focused on older children who were already in preschool. However, the Nagys soon developed a good relationship with a home therapist trained in ABA. She worked closely with Merrill and Raphael, helping them learn how to build Michael's play skills. They learned to watch him at play and to find ways to gradually expand it based on his interests and skills. By working with Michael during play, they also found ways to promote language and social skills.

Introduction

Fortunately for the Nagys, they were able to identify differences in their son's development early so that he could benefit from early identification and services. Learning to intervene with their son at such a young age has allowed them to teach him new skills that will have a big impact on his development. Also, intervening with play skills at such a young age has helped the Nagys to expand Michael's

interests and activities. This makes it less likely that he will continue to maintain his narrow, focused, and repetitive interests over time.

This chapter gives an overview of the importance of play in child development, and a broad blueprint for the range of play skills and behaviors that are common in early childhood. After providing a solid understanding of how and why play develops, the chapter will describe strategies that have been shown to be effective in building play repertoires for young children with autism spectrum disorders.

The Importance of Play

Through play, children develop a number of skills by watching and interacting with toys, other objects, and people around them. Through play-based activities, children expand and develop language, communication, motor, social, and cognitive skills. They learn about concepts such as cause-and-effect, they relate objects and sounds to daily life, and they take part in social exchanges and turn taking.

Generally speaking, play develops in a typical sequence in children, becoming more complex as they grow older. However, for individual children, the development of play interests and behaviors varies quite a bit, depending on their interests, experiences, and environments. The table below gives a general description of the development of the social context of play.

Typical play usually develops hand in hand with a child's social development and social environment. Children often spend more time

Table 7-1	Typical Development of Play Skills	
0–2 Years	Solitary	Children often play alone.
2–2.5 Years	Spectator	Children may observe other children playing but do not play with them.
2.5–3 Years	Parallel	Children play alongside others but not necessarily together.
3–4 Years	Associate	Children start to interact with others in their play and there may be fleeting cooperation. Children develop friendships and preferences for playing with some playmates. Play is normally in mixed sex groups.
4–6+ Years	Cooperative	Children play together with shared goals. As children reach primary school age, play is often in single sex groups.

with brothers and sisters or friends than with adults as they get older, and they become more aware of and interested in other people. Accordingly, play becomes more complex and social as the child develops.

During their earliest months, children spend most of their waking hours interacting with caregivers and with toys and other objects in their immediate environment. As infants, they look at adults and explore toys and objects with their mouth and hands. Toward the end of their first year, their keen awareness of adults leads to imitation of actions and expressions, manipulation of objects, and simple social-action games such as peek-a-boo. During this stage, some of the important achievements mastered through play include the beginnings of joint attention and turn taking, as well as awareness of simple cause-and-effect relationships.

By their second year, most children begin to notice and imitate other children, and repeat favorite actions with objects. As children become mobile and examine their surroundings, they have better motor control for manipulating objects. They also learn how things function through trial and error and can figure out how to activate an interesting toy. This type of play may be repetitive because it is so interesting. Children at this age may also begin using language such as sound effects, exclamations, or words when they play by themselves or with adults. These developments expand the child's basic joint attention and cause-and-effect skills, and set the stage for problem solving skills and increased language skills.

During the toddler and preschool years, children become more interested in playing alongside other children, and they continue to copy adults and also peers. They add actions to their play repertoire which they learn by exploring the environment or by imitating the people around them. At this age, children begin to use items symbolically in play. For example, they may pretend that a bowl is a hat. They also imitate basic actions of daily life such as holding a phone to the ear, using a toy hammer, or stirring in a pot. Play during this timeframe is a way for children to practice everyday activities or things they watch in the world around them, and their play begins to imitate "real life" as they see it.

Over time, typically developing children increasingly use their play skills with other children. They negotiate turn taking and share play scenarios (e.g., playing "cooking"). Later in the preschool years, children expand and develop these themes and actions, and also relate play to more complex daily experiences. For example, they play house or pretend to go to the store, enacting events they remember from their own life. Playing simple games, following rules, and other cognitive learning is noticeable at this stage. Children recognize shapes, letters, and colors, and also attempt to solve puzzles through a mixture of thinking and trial and error.

Even for children who are typically developing, progressing through these stages has challenges. Social negotiation, patience, tolerance, and interests vary dramatically from child to child and even from moment to moment. So even though a child has a particular set of play skills and interests, there is no guarantee that his play interactions will always be successful. Often a child may play well with a playmate in a particular situation but not with his sibling, or vice versa! However, with some parental guidance, children without ASD are generally able to use their social and communication skills to help them navigate play situations.

Play Stages in Children with ASD and Other Developmental Disabilities

There are vast differences in the ways play may be affected for children with ASD. Some children do not play with or interact with toys at all, and instead focus on repetitive actions with their own hands or body. Other children with ASD approach or use toys, but in unusual or repetitive ways, such as spinning them, mouthing them, or repeatedly dropping or throwing them. Other children use toys in more typical ways, but always follow a particular pattern or ritual in their play.

While these differences in play among children with ASD appear very different, the common theme that makes them part of the same diagnosis is this: Their play is not social or reciprocal. In other words, the play does not involve two people taking a role as part of the play, or, if it does involve another person, it is rigid and inflexible (the person always has to do the same thing). Also, the play of children with ASD lacks creativity and flexibility, and does not typically relate to everyday events.

To help your child acquire the basic play skills that typically developing children pick up naturally, it's important to understand how his play may or may not be developing. A researcher named Karen Lifter and her colleagues studied whether children with disabilities

showed similar stages of play development as children without disabilities (Lifter, 2000). Although their research did not focus on ASD exclusively, it provides a detailed starting point to track play milestones. Table 7-2 displays the general categories and descriptions of play that these researchers observed in their extensive study of play behavior in young children with developmental disabilities.

In contrast to the sequence of play skills seen in typical development, the play skills observed by Lifter and her colleagues did not occur in a fixed sequence or at predictable ages. The play behaviors did, however, vary in individual children depending on their other skills and their developmental level.

All of these play stages are stages that typically developing children go through as well. The main difference is that children *without* ASD go through the stages in this specific order and usually at specific ages. Children with developmental disabilities, as studied by Lifter and her colleagues, do not predictably go through each stage or progress in order through the stages, or they may be delayed in their development through the stages.

Even when children with ASD have many of the play skills in this list, it may also be more common for them to stick to certain themes or "pretend" actions that are rigid or to re-create a very specific video or

Table 7-2 | Description of Play Categories in Developmental Sequence (Lifter, 2000)

Play Category	Description
Single Object Actions	*Indiscriminate:* Treats all objects alike (banging, mouthing, throwing) *Discriminate:* Treats objects differently (rolls balls, bangs sticks, squeezes stuffed animals)
Multiple Object Actions (combinations)	Combines items in certain ways: ■ *Takes apart:* Takes puzzle pieces out ■ *Puts together:* Puts puzzle pieces in ■ *General:* Puts block in cup ■ *Specific—Conventional:* Puts cup on saucer ■ *Specific—Physical:* Stacks blocks
Pretend Self	Brings empty cup to mouth to drink
Child as Agent	Extends cup to doll's mouth, combs doll's hair
Single Scheme Sequences	Extends the same familiar action to two or more figures: cup to baby doll; cup to stuffed lamb
Substitutions	Uses one object to stand in place for another; e.g., puts bowl on head for a hat
Doll as Agent	Moves doll figures as if they are capable of action. For example, moves figure to load blocks into a truck, puts mirror into doll's hand to see itself, has animal eat out of bowl
Multischeme Sequences	Extends different actions to same figure. For example, feeds doll with spoon, wipes it with cloth, then puts it to bed
Socio-dramatic Play	Adopts familiar roles in play theme; e.g., plays house; plays beauty shop
Thematic Fantasy Play	Adopts roles of fantasy characters such as Superman

book. They do not have the flexible, creative, or social aspects of play that typically developing children do. For example, a child with ASD may engage in Superman play, but only follow one script and not change it in response to other people's roles or actions. Play of that kind is much harder to identify as a problem than play of children with ASD who are primarily focused on spinning objects or holding them up to their eyes.

Although the study by Lifter and her colleagues provides some insights into the actions and behaviors that children with disabilities use when playing, it does not tell us about the social interactions that occur during play. Some observations about those interactions (not part of Lifter's research) are that children with ASD often remain in the solitary stage for longer than other children do, or progress through the other stages of play in an isolated way, without showing as much creativity or interaction with others during play.

In short, play is the domain that brings together three areas of challenge for children with autism spectrum disorders: social interaction, communication, and restricted or repetitive interests. It's like a triple-whammy! For more description of both social and communication development and how we can address it, review Chapters 5 and 6. Just as it is critically important to begin intervention early and intensively to develop foundation skills in those areas, it is also important to focus on play. Building a solid foundation of common, basic play skills helps equip children with ASD with a set of well-practiced skills that are "ready to go" in situations where the social demands become increasingly complex over time.

Evaluating Your Child's Current Play

In looking over Table 7-2, you may have noted some play actions that your own child does regularly, as well as some he does not do. If you are not sure which of these actions your child does, take some time to assess his current play skills by purposefully watching how he plays with toys and objects. Establishing a list of his current play actions and interests will give you a starting point for intervention. For example, you might observe that your child frequently combines two objects when playing, but only does this with a few toys. If so, you can gradually begin to expand his play. First, you can try to expand the variety of toys he uses by gradually introducing new toys that have similar features to the toys he currently favors. For example, if he uses a spoon to feed a doll, you could teach him to comb the doll's hair. Second, you can try to expand a familiar combination by introducing a new, different looking doll to alter a repetitive combination.

An early intervention therapist can use many different tools to assess your child's play skills and develop goals for play. These assessments should all combine direct observation of your child and reference to some curriculum or play skill sequence. There are many well established curriculum guides for pinpointing play skills that children need to learn and for developing teaching programs. Any therapist who is providing your child with early intervention treatment should have a set of tools that guides her programming.

A few of the common and well-known assessment and curriculum guides that encompass play skills are:

- *Behavioral Intervention for Children with Autism* (Maurice, Green, & Luce),
- *A Work in Progress* (Leaf & McEachin),
- *An Early Start for Your Child with Autism* (Rogers, Dawson, & Vismara), and
- *Assessment of Basic Language and Learning Skills* (Sundberg & Partington).

What these guides have in common is their focus on breaking down play (and other) skills into components and using ABA approaches to teach and systematically build those skills. These books can be very useful resources to parents who are working on play skills in addition to other important skills.

Strategies for Teaching Play

Interventions aimed at teaching young children with ASD new play skills are ideally done in a *natural context*. That means your child will work on play skills using familiar toys and typical play scenarios in settings where children usually play. For example, interventions may take place at his daycare center, or in the family room, bedroom, sandbox, or even the bathtub.

One of the first steps in coaching your child to develop play skills is to identify objects, toys, or activities that he already finds interesting and motivating. Often, it is best to start by addressing play within situations that are already occurring, instead of in a more formal or novel set-up (like sitting at a small desk or table). You can then begin to expand your child's play repertoire by gradually introducing new elements into the established routine. For example, you can show your child how to do something new with a familiar toy, or you can show him how to do a familiar action with a new toy. Let's say that your child plays with trains or cars by turning their wheels or pushing them along the floor. If so, you may be able to intrigue him by creating a ramp out of books and boxes and then watching the car or train whoosh down the ramp. In this example, you are exposing your child to new and fun things to do with objects he already likes as well as helping him learn that *you* brought something new and fun to the play.

It is also important to help your child develop some basic foundation skills that are essential to more learning. These include:

- imitating others' actions,
- imitating object manipulation, and
- imitating sounds or words.

These skills are prerequisites to having your child learn to perform new actions during play, or to imitate a playmate's play actions. For example, a child who often holds a toy cow may be taught with much practice to imitate "moo" when he has the cow. Or he may be taught to put a toy figure in a car, imitating the action of putting one object in another. This action can then be expanded to a wide range of play situations or objects. In these examples, basic foundation skills such as object imitation and vocal imitation are key behaviors that set the stage for more advanced play learning later.

While it is preferable for children to learn how to watch and imitate others' actions using toys *while they are playing*, this strategy does not always work. Some children benefit instead from focusing on these basic skills in a more structured setting and from the use of ABA teaching strategies such as discrete trial instruction (see Chapter 3). This may be the case if the typical play environment is too distracting for a child to focus on what the instructor is doing or if the child has a strong motivation to do different things with the toy. In a basic discrete trial program, this child may be given an object (toy horse), an instruction ("do this"), and a model (the instructor making the horse "gallop"). The child is then given opportunities (or trials) to practice that skill.

After the child learns this new action in an instructional setting, the action can then be introduced during a play setting. When this type of structured learning is used in a less natural environment, it is important to balance the instruction with other natural and less formal teaching scenarios.

Beyond Basic Play

After children with ASD have learned basic play skills such as imitation and are able to play with toys more flexibly, they may be ready to learn more advanced play skills. Research supports the use of several strategies for teaching more advanced levels of play or play sequences, including video modeling, scripts, and sibling coaches.

Video Modeling. Rebecca MacDonald and her colleagues (2005) at the New England Center for Children have used video modeling to teach a number of youngsters with ASD how to play appropriately with common toy sets such as a farm set or a toy castle with royal figures. In video modeling, teachers or parents first videotape other adults or children doing something that they want the child with ASD to do. Then the child with ASD is presented with the same set of toys as seen in the video and is guided in repeating the play that was shown. This type of intervention takes advantage of the fact that some children with ASD naturally show interest in video and may already try to imitate things they see in a video.

In the studies by MacDonald, children with ASD were given opportunities to watch videotapes of play sequences with various toys, and then systematically taught to play in the way that they observed in the video. For example, they were shown a play airport, and a sequence of activities within the airport, such as a plane coming in for a landing, a toy figure fueling the plane, suitcases removed from the plane, and figures of people leaving the plane, etc. The play sequence also includes some language or sound effects ("whoosh!" as the plane is landing, or comments that each character could make such as "time for a fill up!").

A down side to this type of intervention is that it can sometimes lead to a rote type of play (children imitating what they have seen). However, it has also been shown that children who successfully learn these play sequences can often learn to improvise and expand upon them once they are mastered.

There are also several important upsides to using video modeling instruction. First, children with ASD are interested in watching videos and readily imitate the desired actions. Second, video modeling does not require an adult to be involved in the play situation, which can be helpful in many settings where there are peers. If a child can learn a play sequence by watching a video, he may be less likely to rely on an adult's instructions and support while he is playing. Instead, he can simply use the play sequence he has learned in a group with other children. For more information about video modeling, you may wish to refer to *How to Use Video Modeling and Video Prompting* by Jeff Sigafoos, Mark O'Reilly, and Berenice De La Cruz (2007).

Scripts. Teaching play scripts or sequences is another strategy that can help children with autism spectrum disorders learn more advanced play skills. A play script is a sequence of play actions and/or comments that a child can use while he is playing with a certain object or in a certain situation. The main difference between scripts and video modeling is that play scripts are not presented via video. A child may learn a script by practicing with a therapist and memorizing the actions, words, or comments in a play sequence after they are modeled. The instructor uses prompting and reinforcement (as discussed in Chapter 3) to help the child succeed in following the script.

Another method is to teach the child to independently use technology such as a Language Master to play a recording of each step in the script. (A Language Master is a playback device similar to a tape recorder.) For more information about using scripts, see *Teaching Conversation to Children with Autism: Scripts and Script Fading* by Lynn McClannahan and Patricia Krantz (2005).

Like video modeling, play scripts can be helpful because children with ASD often have problems being creative or coming up with a way to use a toy or set of toys. Providing a model or script removes the challenge of figuring out what to do with the toy, enabling the child to focus on using the object appropriately with others. Once a child masters a specific play script, he can then learn to improvise and adapt the play sequence he has learned when he encounters new play activities. For example, initially he might repeat the same sequence every time he plays with the airport toys. Over time, he can be encouraged to imitate new actions (e.g., his mother says, "Do this with the plane" and shows him a flying loop in the air). This line of research is one of many strategies that shows promise in helping children with ASD play in more traditional ways with toys.

Siblings as Coaches. Another area of successful research focuses on involving brothers and sisters in play intervention to help children with ASD learn to play with peers. Siblings are great role models for children with autism, and are often the first and most frequent play partner a child with ASD will have.

A study by David Celiberti and Sandra Harris was very successful in teaching siblings of children with autism to become play coaches for their brother or sister with autism. Siblings were able to teach their brother or sister with ASD to imitate certain toy actions or sounds with objects by getting their brother or sister's attention, using simple instructions ("watch me" or "do this"), and giving clear feedback—"that's it!" or "you did it!" Teaching siblings to act as coaches not only helps children with autism to develop real play skills, but also benefits the siblings who receive training. As a result of training, siblings often feel less frustrated when interacting with their brother or sister or reap other emotional rewards such as feeling empowered and successful as a teacher.

Of course, before you ask your children to learn to coach their brother or sister, make sure they have the interest and motivation to learn these skills. Also consider the specific characteristics of your child with ASD before embarking in this direction. For example, if your child has been making good progress in early intervention with a therapist or adult, introducing a sibling would be a good next step in learning play skills. But if your child is still resisting others' involvement in his play and reacts with frustration or more challenging behavior when interrupted during play, it may be too early to ask siblings to learn how to coach him.

In general, when a young child with autism is receiving home-based intervention, it is very helpful for siblings to become engaged and connected to the process. If your child with ASD has no siblings at home, then a young cousin or a child who lives nearby can assume the role of play coach, if interested, or he or she can be a playmate who helps your child practice his new skills outside of teaching sessions with adults.

Summary

Play, in and of itself, is extremely valuable to teach your child, since play is what children are expected to do for the majority of the time when they are very young. Building a range of appropriate play skills may also help prevent the further development of restricted, repetitive, or isolated interests, as well as other problematic behaviors that interfere with learning and interaction. For young children, play is also the primary means for teaching other communication, social, and cognitive skills. With careful assessment and by systematically building play goals into your child's natural activities and environments, you can help him make significant progress. This, in turn, will help him with all other areas of learning.

Research has shown that the best gains are made when interventions are begun as intensively and as early as possible. Fortunately, teaching play skills does not need to wait until school starts. You and your child can begin this important work right away.

References

Buggey, T. (2009). *Seeing is Believing: Video self-modeling for people with autism and other developmental disabilities.* Bethesda, MD: Woodbine House.

Celiberti, D., & Harris, S. (1993). Behavioral intervention for siblings of children with autism: A focus on skills to enhance play. *Behavior Therapy, 24*(4), 573–599.

Leaf, R., & McEachin, J. (1999). *A work in progress.* New York, NY: DRL Books.

Lifter, K. (2000). Linking assessment to intervention for children with developmental disabilities or at-risk for developmental delay: The developmental play assessment (DPA) instrument. In K. Gitlin-Weiner, A. Sandgrund, & C. Schafer

(Eds.), *Play diagnosis and assessment* (2nd ed., pp. 228-261). New York: John Wiley and Sons.

MacDonald, R., Clark, M., Garrigan, E., & Vangala, M. (2005). Using video modeling to teach pretend play to children with autism. *Behavioral Interventions, 20*, 225-238

Maurice, C., Green, G., & Luce, S. (1999). *Behavioral intervention for children with autism.* Austin, TX: ProEd.

McClannahan, L., & Krantz, P. (2005). *Teaching conversation to children with autism: Scripts and script fading.* Bethesda, MD: Woodbine House.

Partington, J. W., & Sundberg, M. L. (1998). *Assessment of basic language and learning skills* (The ABLLS). Pleasant Hill, CA: Behavior Analysts, Inc.

Rogers, S., Dawson, G., & Vismara, L. (2012). *An early start for your child with autism: Using everyday activities to help kids connect, communicate, and learn.* New York, NY: Guilford Press.

Sigafoos, J., O'Reilly, M., & De La Cruz, B. (2007). *How to use video modeling and video prompting.* Austin, TX: Pro-Ed.

8

Boosting Your Child's Independence: Early Self-Help Skills

The O'Reilly Family

Mary and Liam O'Reilly had four children ranging in age from Patrick, who was 3 years old, to Megan, who was 12. Their household was a lively place. Their three older children had easily learned self-help skills such as toileting and dressing and were motivated to be big girls or big boys who could take care of themselves. Only Patrick, who was diagnosed with autism spectrum disorder (ASD), still needed a great deal of assistance from his parents. He was still in diapers and had to be undressed and dressed because he had no interest in doing it for himself.

Pat was in a private day school for children with ASD. He was making good progress with some of his skills such as establishing joint attention with staff members and following single commands and sometimes two-step commands. At a conference at school, Pat's teacher, Lynne, encouraged Mary and Liam to work on Pat's self-help skills at home. They agreed to do so, but reminded Lynne about all the demands on their time from their other children, as well as from Pat.

Lynne said she respected their situation, but that as Pat became more independent he would need less help from them. She gave them some guidance in teaching self-help skills and told them she would work on the same skills in school whenever Pat needed to get dressed or undressed. For example, she suggested they teach Pat how to pull down and pull up his trousers so that he would already be able to do that once they started toilet training. She also suggested that they make cooperating with dressing part of his daily routine. Lynne told Mary and Liam that Pat was old enough and had good enough motor skills to learn to undress himself. No more just putting clothes on Pat! He would have to become part of the *process. Lynne also taught Pat's parents the basics of using ABA methods to shape and reinforce self-help skills.*

In about a month, Pat mastered several self-help skills—raising his arms to assist with having t-shirts taken off, pulling off his socks when he was being undressed, and pulling down his pants before he sat on the toilet. Then Mary and Liam started toilet training him. They did this in collaboration with Lynne, so that all of the adults were involved in the process of teaching him. Urine training went fairly quickly, as Pat had good bladder control and he could see other boys in his class using the toilet and earning praise for doing a good job. Bowel training was a bit more challenging because Pat rarely gave any cue that he was having a bowel movement and the need did not occur as often. After a few more months, however, he was able to use the toilet at home or at school to have a bowel movement, although he still needed help with wiping himself.

Introduction

The O'Reillys probably took longer than many parents to teach their son to use the toilet, dress and undress, and do other age appropriate self-help skills. As they told Lynne, their lives were very busy with multiple demands. Lynne acknowledged that, but pointed out that there was light at the end of the tunnel. When children learn to dress themselves, use the toilet, wash their hands and face, and brush their teeth, these skills are directly useful to the child, and they also make a parent's life somewhat easier. Lynne was pleased to see that Pat was learning the self-help skills that would allow him to be more independent at school as well as at home

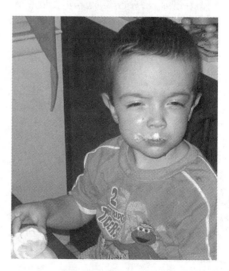

Although many children on the autism spectrum are delayed in learning basic self-help skills, essentially all of them can learn these skills with patient teaching. Because

these activities are so integral to routines at home, parents have many opportunities to support their children in mastering dressing, buttoning, brushing teeth, and so forth. Each time your child gets dressed, washes her hands before she eats, or gets ready for bed, there is an opportunity to insert a brief lesson into the process.

This chapter gives you a few examples of how to teach basic self-help skills to very young children. For a more extensive discussion of teaching self-help skills to children of all ages, you may wish to consult the book by psychologist Stephen Anderson and his colleagues, *Self-Help Skills for People with Autism* (Anderson, Jablonski, Thomeer, & Knapp, 2007). Because of its detailed teaching steps for a multitude of self-help activities, that book will be useful for many years as your child continues to master new skills for independence.

A Couple of General Concepts

The chances that you will succeed in teaching self-help skills will be higher if your child has learned some of the basic attending skills. These include paying attention to you, following simple directions ("sit here"), and imitating your actions ("do this") when you model them. It is also important to identify some potential sources of reinforcement that will motivate your child to cooperate and do the work needed to master the skills you are trying to teach.

See Chapter 3 for a discussion of how to motivate your child to do the work of learning. For a more extended discussion of motivating learners with autism spectrum disorders, see the book *Incentives for Change* by Lara Delmolino and Sandra Harris (2004) in the Woodbine House *Topics in Autism* series.

Milestones for Typically Developing Children

Table 8-1 shows the ages that typically developing children master certain self-help skills. For example, a typically developing two-year-old learns to undress herself and will cooperate with dressing by holding out her arm or foot. The typical three-year-old can take off and put on her coat, and pull up pants with an elastic waistband. By four years of age, children take off most of their clothing independently,

Table 8-1 | Milestones for Self-Help Skills of Typically Developing Children

Eating	
Drinks from a cup with help	around 12 months
Picks up & eats finger food	around 12 months
Eats with spoon (some spilling!)	around 36 months
Eats with fork (some spilling)	around 48 months
Dressing	
Undresses self	around 24 months
Puts on shoes but doesn't tie	around 36 months
Dresses with help	around 36 months
Dresses except for buttoning	36 to 48 months
Buttons & zips	around 48 months
Completely undresses	around 48 months
Dresses & undresses by self	48 to 60 months
Ties shoes	around 60 months
Toilet	
Interest in toilet training	around 24 months
Toilet training achieved	36 to 48 months
Toilets with help	36 to 48 months
Independent at toilet	48 to 60 months
Washes & dries hands	around 36 months
Brushes teeth with help	around 48 months
Speech	
Babbles with "speech" intonation	around 12 months
Able to say first word	around 12 months
Several single words	15 to 18 months
Short phrases	18 to 24 months
Simple sentences	24 to 36 months
5-word (or more) sentences	36 to 48 months
Play	
Parallel play emerges	around 24 months
Enjoys simple puzzles & shapes	around 24 months
Simple pretend play	around 24 months
Increasingly creative play	around 36 months
Pretend social role play	around 36 months
Board games	around 48 months

pull on their socks, and put their shoes on their feet (but do not tie the laces). These dressing and undressing skills, which are listed roughly in order of complexity, are a good place to start in helping your child gain independence in dressing and undressing.

For information on other skills, we recommend the book by Stephen Anderson and his colleagues. It devotes considerable space to teaching parents how to use effective teaching methods to support children with ASD in gaining full independence in dressing and undressing skills.

Dressing and Undressing

Perhaps your child has already learned to pull off her shoes and socks. Many little people delight in their bare toes! If your child does not pull off her socks, it might be a good undressing skill to start with, as many young, typically developing children learn this as one of their first independent undressing skills (Table 8-2).

First, gather some baseline data (discussed in Chapter 3). After you remove your child's shoe, say "sock off" and wait to see if she will take her sock off. She might, but she might not. If she does, give her praise and cuddles for following your direction. If she does not, simply remove the sock for her. This is the "baseline" condition and you want to know what she can do if you simply ask her.

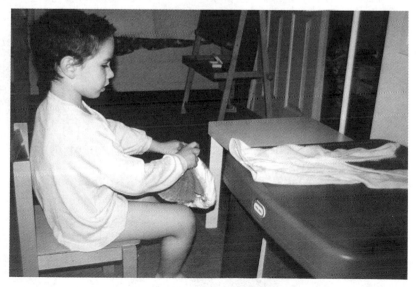

Table 8-2 | Removing Socks

Target Behavior: Teach child to remove socks

Objective: Teach child to pull off her own socks by grasping toe of sock

Say to Child: "Sock off"

Step 1 Baseline	Sock fully on foot	Remove	Tug	No Response	
Step 1 Baseline	Sock fully on foot	Remove	Tug	No Response	
Step 1 Baseline	Sock fully on foot	Remove	Tug	No Response	
Step 1 Baseline	Sock fully on foot	Remove	Tug	No Response	
Step 2	Sock near toes	Remove	Tug	No Response	Prompt Full Part
Step 2	Sock near toes	Remove	Tug	No Response	Prompt Full Part
Step 2	Sock near toes	Remove	Tug	No Response	Prompt Full Part
Step 2	Sock near toes	Remove	Tug	No Response	Prompt Full Part
Step 3	Sock near arch	Remove	Tug	No Response	Prompt Full Part
Step 3	Sock near arch	Remove	Tug	No Response	Prompt Full Part
Step 3	Sock near arch	Remove	Tug	No Response	Prompt Full Part
Step 3	Sock near arch	Remove	Tug	No Response	Prompt Full Part
Step 4	Sock over heel	Remove	Tug	No Response	Prompt Full Part
Step 4	Sock over heel	Remove	Tug	No Response	Prompt Full Part
Step 4	Sock over heel	Remove	Tug	No Response	Prompt Full Part
Step 4	Sock over heel	Remove	Tug	No Response	Prompt Full Part
Step 5	Sock pulled up	Remove	Tug	No Response	Prompt Full Part
Step 5	Sock pulled up	Remove	Tug	No Response	Prompt Full Part
Step 5	Sock pulled up	Remove	Tug	No Response	Prompt Full Part
Step 5	Sock pulled up	Remove	Tug	No Response	Prompt Full Part

If your child does not consistently take her sock off after three or four nights of baseline, it is time to teach her to remove her sock. When you are getting your child ready for bed or a bath, take off her shoes and then pull down one sock so that it is partially off and near her toes. Say, "Sock off." If she makes no move to take it off, take her hand and guide her though pulling off the sock by grasping the toe of the sock. (That is the way most infants and toddlers learn to take off their sock—by the toe and not the heel.) It may work best if you use socks that are relatively loose fitting because they are easy to remove.

When your child tugs the sock off by the toe, she has completed the removal of one sock. Be sure to reward her with praise and perhaps a gentle rub of her toes while you exclaim, "There are your toes!" or something similar. Repeat the routine with the other foot. Do it again the next night and be sure to give your child a little time to try to pull off the sock by herself. If she pulls it off or even tries to, give lots of praise and tummy rubs, tickles, or other reinforcements you have determined are motivating to your child. As your child learns to take off her socks, fade your physical prompts as quickly as possible. Gradually reduce the extent to which you partially pull down the sock.

On your data sheet (Table 8-2), make a record of where you positioned the sock and whether your child needed a full physical prompt or a partial prompt. Do Step 1, the baseline with the sock pulled up on your child's foot. Then, in teaching Step 2, pull the sock down to your child's toes so she can easily pull it off. After several days of success with the sock near her toes, position the sock by your child's arch, then over her heel, and finally pulled up on her ankle. If you need to use a physical prompt, you should circle whether it was a full hand-over-hand prompt or a partial prompt (part).

When your child can take off both socks on her own, you can move on to teaching her to take off her shoes. Follow the same broad script by starting with the shoe partially removed and asking your child to remove it. Again, prompt no more than necessary and be generous in your praise. Your goal is to be able to say to your child "shoes and socks off" before a bath or at bedtime and have her do what you ask. Don't forget the importance of collecting some baseline data and keeping a record of your child's performance with this and every other behavior you teach.

To create more data collection sheets for yourself, follow the model in Table 8-3 on the next page. First name the longer-term target you are aiming to teach. For example, it might be for your child

Table 8-3 | A Generic Data Sheet

Target Behavior: Teach child to cooperate with pulling pants down to ankles

Objective: Teach child to pull down elastic waist pants from below buttocks to ankles

Say to Child: "Pants down"

Date	Condition	Trial 1	Trial 2	Trial 3
8/11	Baseline	0	0	0
8/12	Baseline	0	0	0
8/13	Baseline	0	0	0
8/14	Full prompt	1	1	1
8/15	Full prompt	1	1	1
8/16	Partial prompt	0	1	1
8/17	Partial prompt	1	1	1
8/18	Partial prompt	1	1	1
8/19	Gesture prompt	1	0	1
8/20	Gesture prompt	1	1	1
8/21	No prompt	0	1	1

to cooperate in pulling down her pants. Your first objective might be to teach her to pull her pants down from below her buttocks to her ankles. You can use the signs "+" to indicate your child was able to do the skill and "–" to indicate she was not able to do the skill, or, as shown in the example, a "0" and "1." After you collect the unprompted baseline data, be sure to note the kind of physical or gestural prompt you use to teach the skill.

Putting on a T-Shirt

Cooperating with getting dressed is a skill that typically developing children learn fairly early. For example, they learn to hold up their arms to make it easier for a parent to take off their t-shirt. If your child has learned to imitate or follow directions for some basic body movements such as raising her arms, it may be quite easy to transition this into a bedtime or bath time routine. You can teach her to raise her arms over her head when you say "hands up," enabling you to remove her t-shirt.

If your child has not yet learned to follow the direction "hands up," undressing time is the perfect setting in which to teach her to follow this instruction. First, take a few days of baseline data (Table 8-4) in the area where you usually undress her. See if she will follow the direction without any active teaching on your part. If she does not follow your request during baseline, you will want to use prompting and reinforcement to teach that skill. You can code the failure to respond during baseline as "NR" for "no response." Do not prompt your child during the baseline as you want to know if she can do the skill on her own. The plus during the teaching sessions indicates that she responded when prompted.

As soon as your child can raise her arms over her head in response to "hands up" without any prompts, you should integrate this skill into both dressing and undressing. That is, ask her to put her hands up to help with shirt removal during undressing and putting her shirt on during dressing. You can make the transition from "hands up" to "shirt off" by initially saying "Shirt off. Hands up" and then leaving off "up" and then "hands" (finally just saying "shirt off"). You should work toward being able to just show your child the shirt and her raising her arms without any instruction at all. Table 8-5 on the next page has a sample data sheet.

Table 8-4 | Raising Hands over Head

Target Behavior: Child raises arms when asked to do so. Done in setting where dressing and undressing are usually done.

Objective: Teach child to raise arms.

Say to Child: "Hands up." After 3 baseline trials, model saying "hands up" as you raise your hands and then quickly guide child's arms above head.

Consequence: Praise child and deliver reinforcement.

Date	Condition	Prompt Full	Prompt Partial	Independent
	Baseline			NR
	Baseline			NR
	Baseline			NR
	Hands Up	+		
	Hands Up		+	
	Hands Up			+

Table 8-5	Cooperating with Pullover Shirt

Target Behavior: Child raises arms when asked to do so during dressing & undressing.

Objective: Teach child to raise arms to facilitate putting on or taking off pullover shirt.

Say to Child: "Shirt off (shirt on). Hands up."

Date	Condition	Prompt Full	Prompt Partial	Independent
	Baseline	NA	NA	
	Baseline	NA	NA	
	Baseline	NA	NA	
	Hands Up	+		
	Hands Up	+		
	Hands Up		+	
	Hands		+	
	Hands		+	
	Han			+

Next Steps in Dressing

The sequence of dressing and undressing skills you teach depends in part on the season in which you are teaching. If it is early summer, teaching your child to pull her shorts on and off and cooperating with your putting her t-shirt on and off would be very functional goals.

As fall approaches, you may want to work on having your child cooperate with putting on her coat. Then, when she can do that, work on having her put her coat on by herself. Your child's teacher or home consultant can show you the way many typical children first learn to put on their coat by laying it on the floor and flipping it into position. If your child has trouble buttoning and unbuttoning, you can ask that the skills be added as goals on her IFSP or IEP so that an occupational therapist or physical therapist can do some of the teaching.

Learning to Use the Toilet—Is Your Child Ready?

Most typically developing children begin learning to use the toilet some time after their second birthday and accomplish that skill by the time they are three years old. A few generations back, there was an emphasis on very early toilet training. The older of us, for example, was toilet trained by 9 months of age. However, the younger of us started training her children when they were about 30 months old. Compared to parents 70 years ago, the current generation of parents is much more attuned to the need for their child to be physically ready before toilet training begins. It is useful to know that boys typically gain bladder control later than girls do. So they may be somewhat older before they are ready to learn to use a toilet. If your child with ASD is 30 months or older, she may be ready to learn to use the toilet.

The program we describe here is written to help you determine whether your child has sufficient bladder control to make this important developmental step. If you try to teach her to use the toilet before she has physically matured enough, you will just frustrate yourself and your child.

We are focusing here on the earliest step in toilet training—namely, collecting baseline data to determine whether a child has sufficient bladder control to remain dry for at least an hour. These baseline data will let you know whether attempting toilet training has a chance of success. The book by Stephen Anderson and colleagues (2007) can help you take the rest of the steps to teach independent toileting.

There are *prerequisites for toilet training,* whether a child is developing typically or has ASD. Your child should have sufficient bladder control to keep a diaper dry for at least one hour and she should sometimes wake up dry from her naps. She should also be able to follow your simple instructions, such as "come here," "sit," and "stand up." In addition, she should be able to remain seated on the toilet for a few minutes with some kind of activity to distract her. Ideally, she should have some way to communicate her need for the toilet, whether that is with words, signs, or a picture communication system (e.g.,

PECS; Bondy & Frost, 2001). Being able to communicate will be more important as your child moves toward greater independence, but can be helpful at any stage of toilet training.

Is Your Child Ready for Toilet Training?

- Is your child at least 30 months old?
- Can he/she stay dry for at least an hour during the day?
- Does he/she sometimes wake dry from a nap?
- Can he/she follow basic directions such as sitting on a chair for a few minutes?

Typically developing children are often motivated to learn how to use the toilet by incentives such as getting to wear "big girl" or 'big boy" underwear, earning stickers, and receiving praise and hugs. The notion of "big boy/girl" underwear is much less likely to be motivating for many children with ASD. You will need to identify other objects or experiences that are motivating for your child and reserve them specifically for toilet training. Depending on your child, that could include things such as morsels of a prized food, special toys, or opportunities to watch a short part of a favorite video. If you need to do an assessment to determine what is most motivating for your child, there are suggestions in the book *Incentives for Change* by Lara Delmolino and Sandra Harris (2004) on how to do that evaluation.

Doing a Baseline Assessment of Readiness

The first step is to determine how long your child is likely to remain dry during the day. You can do that by checking her diaper at regular intervals. You might start with 30-minute intervals. If she is rarely dry after 30 minutes, she is not yet ready for training. If she is often dry after 60 minutes, she is probably ready, and if she is dry after 2 hours, then she has quite good bladder control.

Be sure to keep a calm demeanor when doing diaper checks. If your child is wet or has had a bowel movement, change her diaper in a very neutral way without expressing any disapproval. Be pleasant and matter-of-fact about the diaper check.

Don't count on your memory to retain the information about how often your child is dry or wet. Make a chart that shows what time you

Table 8-6 | Toilet Training Readiness Assessment

Target Behavior: Assessing whether the child is ready for toilet training for urine (bowel movements) with adult assistance.

Objective: Determine how long child can remain dry when wearing diaper during the day. Check diaper every half hour during the day.

Say to Child: Every 30 minutes say to your child, "Time to check your diaper." Record your finding. Circle all that apply: Wet, dry, bowel movement.

Time	Status			Today's Date
	Wet	Bowel	Dry	
	Wet	Bowel	Dry	
	Wet	Bowel	Dry	
	Wet	Bowel	Dry	
	Wet	Bowel	Dry	
	Wet	Bowel	Dry	
	Wet	Bowel	Dry	
	Wet	Bowel	Dry	
	Wet	Bowel	Dry	
	Wet	Bowel	Dry	
	Wet	Bowel	Dry	
	Wet	Bowel	Dry	
	Wet	Bowel	Dry	

checked the diaper and circle: Dry, Wet, and/or Bowel (see Table 8-6). If your child's schedule is fairly regular, that will help you narrow your focus so that you know approximately when she is likely to be wet and therefore when you should bring her to the toilet.

Before you start toilet training, you will want 10 to 14 days of baseline (pre-teaching) data so that you have learned the rhythm of your child's elimination pattern. If your child is at home all day every day, then you are the only one who needs to keep records. However, if she goes to school or daycare, or someone else comes in to care for her for part of the day, those other care providers need to keep records

just as you do. Be sure to communicate with them about the importance of keeping baseline data. If your child is in a preschool program, the staff may be willing to collaborate with you in collecting data and planning a training program.

During the baseline period, check your child's diaper when she first wakes up. Note on the chart the time and whether your child was dry, wet, or had a bowel movement (or both urine and a bowel movement). After that, continue to check her diaper every half hour. If your child gives some indication before the 30 minutes are over that she has a wet diaper or a bowel movement, you should check then and make a note of the time.

Bruce Baker, Alan Brightman, and their colleagues (2003) stress that during this baseline phase you should not put your child on the toilet unless you had been doing that prior to collecting the baseline information. If you were already trying to put your child on the toilet, then do make a note of those times when she actually uses the toilet appropriately for either urine or a bowel movement. They also suggest that it may be easier to start training with bowel movements than urine because these happen less often. Bowel movements are also often accompanied by telltale behaviors such as squatting or pushing that clearly indicate what your child is doing. However, like Pat in the opening story, some children give little to no indication when they are having a bowel movement, and some children hide when they are having one.

If your child does not yet show signs of readiness for urine training, wait a few months and then do another 10 to 14 days of baseline data to see whether she has grained greater control in that interval.

If she does show signs of being ready, then buy or borrow one of the books that explain how to teach self-help skills such as toilet training to children with ASD. In addition to the book by Stephen Anderson et al. (2007), Baker, Brightman, and their colleagues (2003) have also written a useful book on teaching a broad array of self-help skills. Both books are available in paperback.

Summary

Collecting baseline data before toilet training and teaching your child to raise her arms so you can take a t-shirt off, are easier than toilet training your child or teaching her to put a shirt on independently. You will want to use one of the very fine books on teaching self-help skills to find programs already written for toilet training, and for mastering the more complicated skills of dressing and other self-help skills such as washing hands and feeding herself. But you will need to know the rhythm of your child's wetting before you can effectively teach toilet training. Similarly, pulling off clothes developmentally precedes dressing and is the place to start with independence in dressing and undressing. You need to set goals for your very young child that are within her motor and cognitive abilities. Teaching very simple skills will be a good step down the road toward greater independence

You will have good partners in teaching self-help skills when your child is in an early intervention program or preschool because most teachers or home consultants know a great deal about teaching these skills. But as a parent, it is important for you to work on self-help skills at home as well, since your child spends a lot of time with you and you have multiple opportunities to teach independence.

References

Anderson, S. R., Jablonski, A. L., Thomeer, M. L., & Knapp, V. M. (2007). *Self-help skills for people with autism: A systematic teaching approach*. Bethesda, MD: Woodbine House.

Baker, B. L., & Brightman, A. J., with Blacher, J. B., Heifetz, L. J., Hinshaw, S. R., & Murphy, D. M. (2003). *Steps to independence: Teaching everyday skills to children with special needs*. 4th ed. Baltimore, MD: Paul Brookes.

Bondy, A., & Frost, L. (2001). *A picture's worth: PECS and other visual communication strategies in autism*. Bethesda, MD: Woodbine House.

Delmolino, L., & Harris, S. L. (2004). *Incentives for change: Motivating people with autism spectrum disorders to learn and gain independence*. Bethesda, MD: Woodbine House.

9

Taking Control of Challenging Behavior and Sensory Problems

The Trevallo Family

Lena Trevallo tried to pretend that she did not notice the disapproving stares of people in the store as she struggled to collect her belongings and maintain control of her two-and-a-half-year-old daughter, Mia. Mia was wailing loudly, red-faced and sweaty, and kept pulling away from her mother and trying to drop to the floor. Stephen and Katie, the older children (ages 7 and 11), stayed close enough to their mom to help if needed, but far enough away to avoid the looks from bystanders. A few kind or understanding onlookers shook their heads, saying "terrible twos!" as if they understood how Lena was feeling.

Back in their minivan in the store parking lot, Lena glanced up at her own red and sweaty face. She had survived the so-called "terrible twos" with Stephen and Katie. But, although those parenting adventures had also been full of frustration and embarrassment, there had been strategies that worked, and things had gotten easier with time.

However, none of the same rules seemed to apply with Mia. Something was different about Mia and her tantrums, as she and Mia's father, Paul, had known for a while. After their daughter's recent diagnosis of ASD, she and Paul were just now beginning to understand the reason behind this difference.

While Lena had always directly addressed her older children's behavior problems, she wished that she could just avoid situations that triggered Mia's behavior problems. When strategies that used to work with her other children failed, Lena felt as if she was at a loss, and she thought it was easier to work around the problems. She also thought that it was fairer to Stephen and Katie just to avoid Mia's outbursts as much *as possible. That way they would not have to feel embarrassed by their sister's behavior.*

Lena felt defeated. Since she and Paul had divorced, she was increasingly having to care for all of her children alone. Paul was attentive and involved, but needed to work long hours to continue to support all of them. Lena's parents tried to help when they could, but they did not understand how to help Mia either. They often told their daughter not to worry—Mia would grow out of these problems. Lena could no longer find much comfort in advice from her friends who were also parents, since they did not understand what she was going through. When they brought up examples of their own children's challenging behavior, Lena just felt as if they were minimizing her problems.

Despite her frustration with Mia's behavior, Lena knew that her daughter was making important progress in skills during her early intervention and speech sessions. What Lena needed was advice about how to work with Mia at home and in the community, as well as effective ways to deal with her behavior problems and extreme sensitivities and rigidities. She decided to ask her home case coordinator to help her better understand and address these ongoing challenges. She also decided to look for a support group so she could network with other mothers who had similar feelings and experiences.

Introduction

All children have challenging behavior at times, and parenting in the best of circumstances is not easy. However, when your child has an autism spectrum disorder, problem behaviors are even more likely. This is due to the specific deficits in language, communication, social interest, and skills that are central to the diagnosis of ASD. These difficulties can make handling behavioral problems even more complex or challenging.

In addition, the narrow, restricted, or repetitive interests of children with ASD may trigger behavior problems in situations that would not trigger problems in typically developing children. Or, these behavior patterns and interests may result in certain behavior problems persisting longer than they usually do in youngsters without ASD.

This chapter will provide an overview of some of the challenging behaviors and sensory issues that may arise and become particularly problematic in young children with ASD. We will review some basic strategies you can use to understand a particular challenging behavior or issue facing your child and family, as well as the basic factors to consider when planning how to address the problem. We will also review many of the strategies that professionals have developed to help parents cope with and address these specific areas of difficulty. These include teaching parents specific skills to use in particular circumstances and providing training that enables parents to develop treatments and plans as their child grows and changes.

Features of ASD Related to Behavior Problems

We have reviewed the core features of autism spectrum disorders throughout the book. But it is useful to take another look at the three main areas here to help you understand why these youngsters so often struggle with behavior and sensory issues.

Communication Deficits. Possibly most important and maybe most obvious is the role that communication difficulties play in the problem behaviors of young children with ASD. All children get frustrated and upset when they cannot let others know what they want or need or cannot explain what is upsetting them. Since most children with ASD are delayed in expressive language, it stands to reason that many resort to less socially acceptable behaviors such as hitting, whining, and crying when they cannot communicate what is on their minds.

To complicate matters, many children with ASD are upset by things that might not upset typically develop-

ing children. This makes it harder for adults to figure out what is wrong. For example, it might be obvious to you that your child is frustrated if he has trouble fitting two pieces of a puzzle together. However, what if your child has a tantrum because there is a small scratch in the surface of one piece—something not noticeable or important to a child without ASD?

Social Interaction Deficits. The problems experienced by children with ASD in developing awareness and reciprocity in their social interactions also play an important part in behavioral difficulties. Consider how quickly typically developing children learn how to respond to a parent's disapproving look. After a period of learning, most children are eager to earn praise and smiles from their parents, rather than stern looks or reprimands.

But when children on the autism spectrum experience social disapproval for challenging behavior, it may not dissuade them from using the behavior again. Or parental disapproval may be no competition for the rewards the child gets from his behavior. For example, a young child who enjoys gazing at his fingers or repetitively waving bits of yarn or thread may not respond to his mother's requests to stop. This may be because he isn't aware of his mother's wishes or isn't concerned about how his parents feel about his behavior. He could also persist in a challenging behavior because he isn't bothered by, or is actually interested in, negative attention or the reaction he gets for that behavior. For example, he may have learned that when he bites his little sister, he gets a reaction from her that he can't get any other way.

Of course, this type of interaction is not unique to children with ASD. Typically developing children sometimes use behavior to get certain types of reactions or attention, as well. However, the main point is that the social aspect of challenging behavior in ASD is less predictable than it is in typical development, and needs to be carefully considered in each situation.

Restricted Interests and Repetitive Behavior. This third area refers to the fact that children with ASD often have very specific or intense areas of focus or interest. These can involve unusual things (hinges or drains), certain types of sensory interests (smells or textures), or more common things (buses, trains, dinosaurs). In any case, these interests really stand out from other childhood interests because of their intensity and their tendency to interfere with the child's ability to develop a range of other interests. For example, a child might become fixated on watching cabinet and door hinges, and have a tantrum if prevented from closing a cabinet in a particular way.

These interests and repetitive behaviors can be problem behaviors in and of themselves, as they might be annoying to others (e.g., a screeching noise the child makes) or dangerous (e.g., an interest in climbing up on high things or trying to examine trucks close up, even if they are speeding down the road). In addition, these interests can also lead to problem behaviors if the child reacts badly when someone tries to get him to stop.

You may be thinking that seemingly unusual or intense interests are a part of many children's personalities as they are growing up. And some researchers (Richler, Bishop, Kleinke, & Lord, 2007) have confirmed that unusual interests and "compulsive behaviors" appear in many children as they develop. The main difference, however, is that in typically developing children, these unusual interests are only present for relatively brief periods of time and eventually fade away or develop into more socially acceptable or shared interests.

A General Approach for Addressing Behavior Problems

Basic Strategies

Understanding the Motivation

Understanding why children engage in a particular behavior when they do is an important first step in addressing the behavior. Often, parents have the best information about when and why their child behaves a particular way. Sometimes behaviors are problematic because of their very nature (e.g., hitting, biting, or screaming). Other times behaviors are problematic because of the context in which they occur. For example, laughing, running around, or spinning may be appropriate behaviors on the playground, but not at the grocery store or in church. Also, these behaviors may be a problem if they occur during times when the child could be learning or using other appropriate behavior such as playing a game or coloring.

To figure out the motivation for a behavior, it helps to ask questions such as when does this behavior *always* happen, or when does this behavior *never* happen. The answers can provide important clues to understanding the context that *sets the occasion* for the behavior. A careful analysis of the things that happen right before or after an instance of behavior help us develop a good guess for why the behavior occurs.

ABC Data. One helpful tool you can use to pinpoint when and why a behavior occurs is an A-B-C data sheet (Antecedent-Behavior-Consequence). This data sheet helps you organize information to develop a beginning treatment plan. Specifically, you look at:

A. What happens before the behavior (the antecedent)?

B. What happens during the behavior or what does the behavior consist of?

C. What happens as a result of the behavior (consequence)? Some common consequences may be that the child receives attention, is given an item or access to an activity, or is able to avoid something he doesn't want to do.

For example, you might notice when taking some ABC data that the behavior always occurs when an activity needs to end (A), and that if your child screams and protests (B), that the change in activity is delayed (C). For an example of an A-B-C data sheet, see Table 9-1.

Assessment Tools. In other situations, it may be harder to figure out a child's motivation for using a particular behavior. Researchers V. Mark Durand and Daniel Crimmins developed a tool called the *Motivation Assessment Scale (MAS)* to help caregivers understand the various motivations (or functions) of behavior through a question and answer format. This checklist was the result of some published research and also has led to ongoing refinement of strategies to help understand problematic behavior in autism. The MAS or other similar tools are a good way to get the process started, and can often provide enough information in a particular situation to develop preliminary treatments.

For a copy of the MAS or another assessment that might be useful, parents should ask their early intervention provider, their child's teacher or behavior analyst, or another professional. For more complex or serious behavior, more involved strategies might be needed (more on that later this chapter).

Automatically Reinforcing Behaviors. Sometimes it is harder to make a guess about the function of a behavior by looking at the ABC information. Some behaviors of children with ASD do not produce obvious effects on the environment. These behaviors include hand flapping, rocking back and forth, running around, spinning, or gazing at things in odd ways, such as from the corner of the eye. In many of these cases, a child may get some sort of sensory information or feedback from his body. In these situations, the behaviors are often referred to as being *automatically reinforcing* (producing their own reinforcement) or *self-stimulatory* (creating sensory stimulation, such as when someone hums to himself or picks at his fingernails). Behaviors that fall into this category may seem different by nature, since they do not appear, on the surface, to have a communication or social function.

Children with ASD are much more likely than other children to do these sorts of behaviors and to value sensory feedback more than other types of feedback (e.g., social feedback). For example, a typically developing child may spin or hum or run back and forth to entertain himself, but will probably stop or prefer to spend time playing with Dad if that option is available. In contrast, a child with ASD may prefer the sensory feedback and isolated action of spinning to social interaction with another person. When a child with ASD values this type of sensory consequence, he is very likely to resist or get upset when someone tries to make him stop.

Building Replacement Skills

Once a reason for the behavior has been suggested, the next step is to figure out an alternative behavior that your child can use to achieve the same outcome. For example, you may have determined that your child uses challenging behavior to get a break from sitting at the dinner table or playing a structured game. Saying "break" or asking for a break with a picture exchange or a sign are appropriate behaviors your child could learn to use instead. (See Chapter 6 for information about choosing a type of communication to teach.)

It is important to evaluate your child's skills to see whether he already has another skill that is equally or even more effective in getting the same outcome as the problem behavior. For example, if your child can say "help" or "I need a break," your job is to figure out why he resorts to screaming or hitting rather than using the language he has. Many times, this is because the problem behavior *works better* than the language, from the child's perspective. He may get help more quickly or avoid a situation more readily if he screams rather than asks.

However, very often, children with ASD do not have an appropriate way of accomplishing what their challenging behavior gets them—which is why they end up using the problem behavior to begin with. If this is the case for your child, it is essential to identify and teach a replacement skill that will let him achieve what he wants as quickly and successfully as the undesirable behavior does. For example, the replacement behavior for a child who screams to get what he wants could be learning an appropriate way to ask with words, pictures, or signs.

When first teaching a replacement behavior, it is important to make sure your child gets what he wants as soon as he even approximates asking appropriately and to give him the prompts he needs to suc-

ceed in asking. This is so he can quickly learn that asking works as well as—or even better than—screaming (or whatever his challenging behavior is). While he's learning to use the replacement behavior, it is also important not to give him what he wants when he uses the problem behavior while you are helping him get what he wants. (Behavior analysts use the terms differential reinforcement and extinction to refer to this process.) Much more detail about this strategy and its success can be found in the ABA research literature or in books such as *Functional Behavior Assessment for People with Autism: Making Sense of Seemingly Senseless Behavior* (2006) or *Stop That Seemingly Senseless Behavior!* (2008).

It is also possible to teach replacement behaviors for spinning or flapping or other actions that seem to be automatically reinforcing. One way is to provide your child with toys that produce similar sensations but that can be used more appropriately and in social contexts. For example, a child who spends a lot of time spinning the wheels on toy cars and watching them may learn to enjoy helicopters with spinning propellers, tops that spin, or other toys that have gears, cogs, and wheels that are meant to be turned. Building replacement skills of this kind involves providing frequent opportunities to learn how to use the new toys and experience their sensory aspects. This takes time, since the child has more experience with spinning the car wheels or flapping his hands.

The types and complexity of replacement skills vary according to the situation; just some basic examples are discussed here. It will be essential to work with a behavior analyst or teacher to identify the elements that are important to your child and family.

Which Behaviors Need Your Attention?

Mild Behavior Problems. Some young children with ASD have only relatively mild behavior problems such as having brief tantrums or refusing to cooperate with some requests. Some repetitive behaviors such as lining things up or only wanting to talk about dinosaurs could also be considered mild problems if they don't take up all of your child's time or result in serious tantrums when interrupted. When behavior problems are mild, you need not be in a hurry to deal with them. Once your child is receiving an effective intervention program and learning important communication skills, his behaviors may become less of an issue over time.

If these mild behavior problems persist, your child's teacher(s) can suggest some ways to address them in a positive fashion. For example, it may help to increase the reinforcement for replacement behavior. You will want to collect baseline data (pretreatment data) over the course of three or four days to find out how often the behavior occurs. Table 9-1 on the next page shows an example of a record sheet that can be used to keep track of the information.

After you know the baseline frequency, you and the teacher can design a program to reduce the behavior, and a data system to help you monitor the effectiveness.

Behaviors That Interfere with Daily Life. Sometimes a child with ASD may have behaviors that are not particularly dangerous but interfere with his family's daily life. For example, like Mia in the story above, a child may have tantrums in stores or other public places, making it difficult for parents to run errands, take their other children to social or sports activities, or enjoy family outings such as trips to a restaurant.

In these types of situations, the first step is to pinpoint an underlying issue for the specific behavior problem, as described in "Un-

Table 9-1	A-B-C Data Sheet		
Date _____			
Time	**Antecedent**	**Behavior**	**Consequence**

derstanding the Motivation," above. For example, in Mia's case, her parents/teachers might find that she seems to have tantrums when she sees something in stores that she wants, or that the noise in stores bothers her so she wants to leave.

Once you have an idea what is behind your child's behavior, you can put together a plan to change the behavior and give your child more skills to be successful. You might choose a goal to begin working on, such as going to a grocery store or restaurant. Ideally, you can work with a teacher or therapist to build a program for your child to learn to tolerate trips to the store or a restaurant, by breaking the event into small pieces of behavior to be learned and practiced systematically. For example, a trip to the store might be broken down into a number of smaller goals. The first goal might be walking into the store and walking back out without having a tantrum. Once your child does that successfully a number of times, the goal might be to walk into the store to purchase one thing near the front of the store, and so on over time.

Serious Behavior Problems. If your child's behavior problems are more serious and could conceivably result in injury to himself or others, you may need to consult with a Board Certified Behavior Analyst (BCBA) who has a deep understanding of applied behavior analysis. He or she will know how to do a functional behavior assessment (FBA) to identify what is maintaining the challenging behavior over time. The behavior analyst will also know how to choose substitute behaviors that may reduce the frequency of the disruptive behavior.

A functional behavior assessment is designed to answer the question of why the child continues to engage in a particular behavior and what alternatives could be provided that would be more reinforcing than the problematic behavior. For example, by using functional communication training (described by researchers Edward Carr and V. Mark Durand in 1985), you could teach your child to hand you or touch a picture that shows him asking for more of his favorite food.

You can find a Board Certified Behavior Analyst to work with by asking for referrals from other professionals who work with your child and family, or by searching the BACB website registry for certified providers (www.BACB.com). Some insurance companies are also establishing networks that include BCBA service providers. For more information about FBA, you may wish to consult the Woodbine House books *Functional Behavior Assessment for People with Autism: Making Sense of Seemingly Senseless Behavior* by Beth Glasberg (2005).

While a young child who has dangerous behaviors is still learning replacement behaviors, it will take a lot of close supervision and guidance to keep him and other family members safe. In the short term, this may mean you need to find extra help with childcare, especially if you are a parent home alone with more than one child. Understandably, this prospect can be daunting, and intensive intervention that is overseen by a behavior analyst may seem all-consuming at first. It may help you to keep in mind, however, that this intervention can set the stage for meaningful, long-term changes in your child's behavior.

Problem Behaviors and Medical Issues. *A note of caution:* Researchers (Rogers & Dawson, 2010) have found that some potentially dangerous behaviors that begin suddenly may reflect a physical problem. For example, if your daughter, who has no history of self-injury, begins to hit her jaw, it may be because she has a dental problem. Or if your son presses or pushes objects into his stomach, he may be feeling pain or discomfort there. Consult your child's pediatrician or dentist if your child abruptly begins a behavior that involves part of his body.

Researchers have also learned that sometimes a challenging behavior has its roots in a physical problem that no longer exists. For example, a child with ASD may start hitting his head when he has an ear infection. If he does not have good communication skills, hitting his head may be the way he communicates his discomfort or displeasure or tries to get his parents' attention. Sometimes the behavior problem may persist after the physical cause has gone away. If you suspect that your child is engaging in a behavior like this, you should discuss and evaluate possible physical causes. If medical reasons are ruled out with help from a pediatrician or other doctor, you can work with a behavior analyst to help identify what events in the environment are *currently* maintaining the behavior, even if they weren't part of why the behavior began in the first place. This would be done by careful observation and A-B-C data, as described above.

Parent Training

Fortunately, while professionals and researchers have been working for years to develop strategies to teach important skills and decrease problem behavior for children with autism, the methods for making these treatment strategies accessible and successful for parents have also improved with time.

Many researchers have shown that parents can learn to assess the factors involved in their child's behavior and to arrange the environment to help build replacement skills. In addition, parents can become well-versed in the principles underlying the various ABA treatment strategies—which enables them to develop behavior change strategies and also help their children develop skills in communication, social behavior, and other areas. Often, parents receive important support and training to learn these skills in groups or through individual consultation with a therapist or behavior analyst. This behavioral parent training is often an integral component of early intervention.

You should not think of parent training as being for people who don't know how to parent. For example, Lena had been very successful in managing the behavior of her other children, but felt at a loss when she tried to apply the same strategies to Mia. The fact is, in typical parenting, you can rely on your child's communication and social relatedness, and an understanding of things that are meaningful and motivating to children. When your child has a diagnosis of ASD, however, those principles don't apply.

Aside from producing clear changes in the behavior of the child with ASD, parent training has also been shown to increase parents' own feelings of effectiveness. In addition, when parent training in behavior assessment and treatment strategies takes place in groups, there are often added benefits. For example, parents can often develop a support network or learn how other parents are coping with similar situations. This support can also help reduce feelings of being isolated or unsupported that plague many parents of young children with ASD.

Because research has long established that parent training and involvement is critical to the success of treatment for children with ASD, you should expect your child's ABA team or EI team to offer you parent training. You should also expect to be part of the treatment itself. If you are working with a professional but feel confused, inept, or frustrated when trying to use the intervention strategies, you should actively ask for training to help you. Some parents might prefer training that involves role play, active modeling, and feedback. In other words, you can ask to have a therapist watch you work with your child and offer you suggestions in the moment.

Summary

Thanks to decades of work and research with young children with autism, we know that significant improvements in behavior and sensory issues are very likely if we intervene early. We also know that special interests and behaviors are likely to come and go throughout a child's life, as he or she grows and changes. It is vital for you to recognize how the features of ASD set the stage for these bumps in the road, and also to know how applied behavior analysis can equip you, the parent, to tackle new challenges as they arise over time.

References

Carr, E. G., & Durand, V. M. (1985). Reducing behavior problems through functional communication training. *Journal of Applied Behavior Analysis, 18*, 111-126.

Durand, V. M., & Crimmins, D. B. (1988). Identifying the variables maintaining self-injurious behavior. *Journal of Autism and Developmental Disabilities,18*, 99–117.

Glasberg, B. A. (2006). *Functional behavior assessment for people with autism: Making sense of seemingly senseless behavior.* Bethesda, MD: Woodbine House.

Glasberg, B. A. (2008). *Stop that seemingly senseless behavior!* Bethesda, MD: Woodbine House.

Richler, J., Bishop, S. L., Kleinke, J. R., & Lord, C. (2007). Restricted and repetitive behaviors in young children with autism spectrum disorders. *Journal of Autism Developmental Disorders, 37*, 73–85

Rogers, S. J., & Dawson, G. (2010). *Early Start Denver Model for young children with autism.* New York, NY: Guilford Press.

10

You Don't Have to Do It Alone: Support for Parents and Other Family Members

The Rosen Family

Learning that their son, David, had an autism spectrum disorder was devastating to Paula and Joe Rosen. They had shared so many dreams about who he would become and how proud they would be of the son they were raising. David was their only child, and, because of the difficult pregnancy Paula had undergone, their physician had advised them not to have any more children.

Paula and Joe got the diagnosis of autism spectrum disorder when their pediatrician administered a routine screening questionnaire at David's regular 24-month checkup. After that, they were caught up in a whirlwind of other consultations to confirm the diagnosis and find resources, and they struggled to accept that not only did David have ASD, but he also appeared to have a significant intellectual delay. Their dreams might never become realities.

Paula and Joe were both overwhelmed by feelings of loss about what might have been, and they grieved for the son they never had. Joe worked long hours and ignored David most of the time when he was home. Paula dragged through her days. She took David to his appointments, but was never really able to work with him at home the way the professionals worked with him in his early intervention program.

David had been named to honor the memory of Paula's father, who died before the baby was born. It was now intolerable to Paula to think that her son could never really honor the memory of her father. What a hollow legacy. After a few months of pain and of feeling isolated from her husband, Paula realized that she had to get her life back on track. She made an appointment to talk to the psychologist who had been part of the team that evaluated David. This was a wise decision.

The psychologist reassured Paula that many parents go through a painful period while they are struggling to accept their child's diagnosis. He suggested several options to help her cope. One was to join a support group for parents of infants, toddlers, and preschool-aged children who had an ASD or appeared to be on track for that diagnosis by the time they were three. Alternatively, she could see an individual therapist at the Center who could help her with the pain she was experiencing. Both were reasonable strategies to try, and she could make her own decision about which path to take.

That evening Paula talked to Joe about how difficult the past few months had been for her and how she missed being able to talk with him about her feelings. She said she sometimes felt like a single mother trying to raise David by herself. It was a long and difficult, but loving conversation, and it helped them both understand each other better. They agreed that whatever Paula wanted to do, they should do together. Reconnecting with each other and coming to this mutual decision was the most comforting thing that had happened to either of them in several months.

Introduction

The Rosens are not unique. Most parents struggle to come to terms with their child's diagnosis on the autism spectrum. Because

Paula and Joe were both fundamentally psychologically healthy people, they finally hit upon an approach that would ease their pain and allow them to help David make the most of his potential.

None of us is an island. We all need loving support and practical help from our families, our friends, and our community, including the professionals who work with us, in educating and caring for our child with ASD. Raising a child with ASD is an unexpected and stressful challenge for families. That stress is especially difficult to manage for parents who have recently received the diagnosis. Often they are still struggling to understand and accept this troubling news and to find the treatment resources their child needs. Because of the nature of ASD, parents of children on the spectrum are more likely to experience stress and depression than are parents of children with Down syndrome or other developmental problems (e.g., Glasberg, Martins, & Harris, 2006; Hayes & Watson, 2013).

If you just got an early diagnosis of an ASD, you may have been told how fortunate you are to find out so soon and to be able to intervene quickly in your child's life. That is true, but the information has also cast you into an entirely new world of early intervention. There are service providers to contact, treatment schedules to arrange, teaching programs to carry out, laundry to wash, and groceries to buy. There are also other family members who need your attention, and periods of anguish when you worry about your child's future and whether you are making the right choices. In two-parent families, one of you may stop working outside of the home in an attempt to better meet the needs of your young child with ASD. In most families, that person is the mother, although some fathers also take on that role. In a single parent family, finding enough human resources can be very daunting.

If you have depended on two incomes to support your lifestyle, your family may now have to redirect some of its financial resources to purchase services for your child, and you will have to do more with less. And through all of this, you will be struggling to accept that the child you love and have invested so many of your dreams in has a very serious developmental disorder. The time just after a child's diagnosis can be a very painful interval when it feels as though your life has been turned upside down. You may well feel all alone in your struggles to cope, but once you start looking for resources, you will probably find there are caring people around you who want to help.

The Burden of Stress

Raising a child with ASD brings with it inevitable stress. Parents can experience stress both mentally and physically. Some of the psycho-

logical responses include sadness, worry, tension, and anger. Physically, parents may experience headaches, fatigue, problems with sleep, loss of appetite, and other kinds of physical discomfort. Some stress is acute in nature. That is, it is painful for a while, but it eventually passes. Other stress tends to be more chronic and to linger over time. Parents who have just learned their child has ASD may experience fairly intense, acute stress in the period right after the diagnosis. As time passes, this stress may diminish in intensity, but a low level of distress may linger over the years and intensify when significant problems occur.

Ironically, at a time when you would really benefit from the support of family and friends, you may be so busy meeting the needs of your child and your immediate family that you don't have much time for those other important relationships. The very people who might help reduce your stress by providing emotional and practical support may be hard to connect with due to the multiple demands on your time.

Reaching Out

Because family relationships and friendships are such a vital source of support, it is essential to find ways to remain connected with the people you love. You might try resolving to pick up the phone at least once a day and call a friend or family member, just to talk or to ask for a favor. Some parents feel embarrassed by their child's unusual behaviors and are reluctant for other people to find out how challenging their child's behavior has become. Start by reaching out to someone you really trust and acknowledge that you need support. If your close family or good friends do not yet understand what you are going through, it is important to tell them about your challenges so that they know how to be helpful. Over time, they can be a big help in reducing your stress.

Your parents, in-laws, siblings, and good friends can all help with practical matters such as taking your typically developing child out for the day, picking up groceries, watching your child with ASD while you take a break, and so forth. They can also support and nurture you on sad days. Don't let a sense of shame or embarrassment keep you from connecting with people who can offer you love and tangible support.

You may also develop friendships with parents of other children with ASD. These friendships can be extremely helpful in part because other parents are also "walking the walk" of raising a child with similar problems. One place to build such relationships is in a parent support group. These groups may be offered at your child's early intervention program, by your local chapter of an autism advocacy group, or by a social service agency in your area. You can also ask the consultant who provides your in-home program, your pediatrician, or your child's teacher about places that offer support groups in your area. An on-line search for "support groups for parents of children with ASD" will also turn up a great many responses. See also the resources listed at the end of this chapter.

It is important to know that research shows that many families who are facing the stress of raising a child with an ASD are able to think about the demands in their lives as challenges and not as a catastrophe. These parents alter their sense of what is most important in their lives and focus their energy on their families and their relationships, and, sometimes, their religious or spiritual values (Glasberg, Martins, & Harris, 2006). The more effectively families cope with the demands in their lives, the less stressful their lives become.

Two Kinds of Coping

There are two broad categories of coping methods—"instrumental" coping and "palliative" coping. Instrumental coping involves taking specific steps to solve the problems you and your family face. That includes finding the right early intervention program for your child, learning the skills of ABA, and reaching out to family and friends for tangible support such as helping you care for your child. In contrast, palliative coping involves finding ways to address your feelings about your child and your family's needs. That includes such things as joining support groups, drawing on your religious or spiritual values, and

seeking emotional support from people you love.

Using the methods of ABA to teach your child new skills and manage her behavior problems will help you feel more effective as a parent. Learning to be an effective advocate for your child in an early intervention or school program also requires instrumental coping skills that allow you to develop the resources your child needs and help you feel effective in your parenting role.

Another instrumental coping method is asking friends to pick up groceries for you each week or to drive your typically developing child to dance or karate classes. Parents are often amazed to discover how willing other people are to lend a hand when they are asked. Other people may not know what you need until you ask, but they are often very glad to help when they understand what you need. If you feel shy about asking, you will need to push yourself a bit to be more assertive about asking for this practical support. One of the best ways to draw on the good will of your family, friends, and neighbors is to come up with a large group of potential helpers and not rely too heavily on any one person. Rotate your requests for help among several different people.

Palliative coping is also important. That involves the emotional support you can get from your partner, your best friend, your siblings, and other parents who have a child with ASD. Being able to pick up the phone and talk to someone you trust can make a big difference. If you are married, your husband or wife may be your best source of emotional support. If you are not supporting each other, you need to talk to one another about that problem. If one of you is too angry, sad, or overwhelmed, you may need to consult a therapist or your religious advisor for help in getting beyond those feelings so that you are able to support one another. If your marriage is strong and you can share your love, you are likely to find the inner strength you need to cope with the demands of raising your child with ASD. Keeping any marriage strong requires continuing work and making time to have good times with each other or simply to be together. Good communication with your life partner is one of the most potent coping tools you have; do all you can to ensure that love remains strong and vibrant.

People who cope well typically have a set of values, often of a religious or spiritual nature, that they rely on to sustain their effort. Although faith is an important aspect of the value system for many people who cope well, that does not necessarily mean they are active members of an organized religion. Rather, it means that they have a set of organizing values or beliefs that they follow. They also see life's challenges as opportunities to accomplish things that matter, and they have a sense of control over their own lives (Glasberg, Martins, & Harris, 2006).

Table 10-1 | Ways of Coping

Examples of Instrumental Coping

- Ask a close family member to stay with the children one evening a week so you and your partner can go out to dinner.
- Learn the fundamentals of ABA so you can apply them to teach your child new skills that will increase her independence.
- Learn enough about education law to ensure that your child's rights are being protected.
- Ask a close family member to do your grocery shopping.
- Ask a good friend to drive your typically developing child to her after school activities one afternoon a week.

Examples of Palliative Coping

- Share your concerns with your partner, best friend, and/or another adult friend.
- Join a parent support group.
- Draw on your personal value system or faith to gain the strength you need.
- Make sure you find some time for yourself and some time with your partner.
- Enjoy your typically developing children.
- Find ways to have family fun with your child with ASD (hiking, riding bikes, taking walks).
- Laughing and smiling make us feel better, so find things to laugh and smile about!

Respite as a Resource

No matter how well you cope from day to day, you still need occasional breaks from your childcare responsibilities. That may involve a few hours each week when you can go off on your own while your partner, one of your parents, or a friend looks after the children. It may also involve a paid respite worker who comes on a regular basis to give you some personal time. Every state in the United States has some form of respite service, whether it is provided through their state-wide services for people with developmental disabilities or a private, not-for-profit agency, or both. This respite may be available free of charge for qualifying families, or offered on a sliding fee basis. See the end of this chapter for examples of links to websites regarding respite care and family support.

Respite care may also be available from staff members at the program that serves your child and your family. Sometimes staff members want to earn extra money and would be very willing to spend a few hours a week or even a weekend staying with your child from time to time.

Some parents also trade weekends with another family who has a child with ASD. One weekend, both children would be with you and you would have a very busy weekend. But another week, it would be your turn to have your child stay with the other family and then you could have a couple of days with a much more relaxed pace of life.

However you can create it, respite is a very important way to sustain yourself in the work that is required a raise a child with ASD. If you don't take good care of yourself, your relationship with your partner, and your relationship with your other children, it will be very difficult to sustain your efforts on behalf of your child with ASD.

Finding Medical and Educational Information

One of the blessings of the Internet is the ability to access a lot of information about autism spectrum disorder very quickly. One of the curses of the Internet is the ability to access a lot of information about autism spectrum disorder very quickly. Blessing and curse. It can be both. For example, several researchers (DiPietro, Whiteley, Mizgalewicz, & Illes, 2013) found that a majority of statements on advocacy sites about the safety and benefits of treatments for ASD and other serious developmental conditions were not based on empirical evidence. The challenge for users is to know what is accurate, what is outdated, and what is not true. Anyone with an opinion can post it on the web and it will be read by others. Remember, you are searching for knowledge, not self-promotion or other people's ignorance.

Clearly, you have to be a savvy reader to separate the wheat from the chaff when you go online to learn about ASD and search for services. Fortunately, there are some resources that are widely respected and trusted, and those should be the focus of your search. There is a list at the end of this chapter of some websites that may be useful to you in locating family support.

Perhaps one of the best ways to find medical and educational services is the old fashioned way of asking the professionals who gave you your child's diagnosis. They are familiar with the resources in your state and know the reputations of many of the service providers. They will know about early intervention services for children under three years of age, and about how to connect with preschool and school-aged services for children over three years in your community. They may be able to suggest a pediatrician and a dentist who are especially good with children with ASD. Asking parents you meet in local support groups or at school can also be a good way to find health care providers who work well with kids with ASD.

Summary

Coming to terms with a diagnosis of ASD in your child is a daunting challenge. You need to find treatment resources, meet the continuing needs of the rest of your family, and somehow make a space for yourself. Your family and friends are likely to rally around you, however, if you can tell them very clearly what you need. Some people say that having a child with ASD made their marriage stronger and some say it increased the distance between them and their partner. You need to keep some space for connecting with your partner and sustaining the good things in your life. You also need to find a way to support your other children in adapting to the needs of their brother or sister with ASD. You will probably be most successful at balancing everyone's needs if you make sure you have enough personal space to nurture yourself.

References

Clifford, T., & Minnes, P. (2013). Who participates in support groups for parents of children with autism spectrum disorders? The role of beliefs and coping style. *Journal of Autism and Developmental Disorders, 43,* 179-187.

Di Pietro, N., Whiteley, L., Mizgalewicz, A., & Illes, J. (2013). Treatments for neurodevelopmental disorders: Evidence, advocacy, and the Internet. *Journal of Autism and Developmental Disorders, 43*, 122-133.

Glasberg, B., Martins, M., & Harris, S. L. (2006). Stress and coping among family members of individuals with autism. In G. Baron, J. Groden, & L. Lipsett (Eds.). *Stress and Coping in Autism* (pp. 277-301). New York, NY: Oxford University Press.

Hayes, S. A., & Watson, S. (2013). The impact of parenting stress: A meta-analysis of studies comparing the experience of parenting stress in parents of children with and without autism spectrum disorder. *Journal of Autism and Developmental Disorders, 43*, 629-642.

Respite and Other Family Support Resources

ARCH National Respite Network and Resource Center has a list of respite services by state at http://archrespite.org/state-respite-coalitions.

The Autism PDD Support Network (www.autism-pdd.net) has helpful information about respite services at www.autism-pdd.net/respite.html.

Parent Centers are funded through the U.S. Department of Education's Office of Special Education Programs (OSEP) to provide information and support to families of children with disabilities. Links to each state's center(s) are at: www.parentcenternetwork.org/parentcenters.html

Specialized Training of Military Parents (STOMP) offers parent training and information for active duty members of the military who have children with disabilities: www.stompproject.org

Local chapters of the **Arc, Easter Seals,** and **United Cerebral Palsy** often offer respite services and/or other types of parent support for families who have children with disabilities. You can locate the nearest chapter of these organizations at:

www.thearc.org
www.easterseals.com
www.ucp.org

Index

About the Authors

Lara Delmolino is Clinical Associate Professor at Rutgers University, and Director of the Douglass Developmental Disabilities Center. She is a Board Certified Behavior Analyst.

Sandra Harris is a Board of Governors Distinguished Service Professor Emerita at Rutgers University, and Executive Director of the Douglass Developmental Disabilities Center.